WORLD BIBLIOGRAPHICAL SERIES

General Editors:
Robert L. Collison (Editor-in-chief)
Sheila R. Herstein
Louis J. Reith
Hans H. Wellisch

VOLUME 5

Saudi Arabia

Frank A. Clements

Librarian and Co-ordinator of Resources,
College of St. Mark and St. John, Plymouth

Saudi Arabia

CLIO PRESS

OXFORD, ENGLAND · SANTA BARBARA, CALIFORNIA

British Library Cataloguing in Publication Data

Clements, Frank
   Saudi Arabia. – (World bibliographical series; vol. 5).
   1. Saudi Arabia. – Bibliography
   I. Title II. Series
   016.953'8   Z3026

   ISBN 0-903450-15-1

Designed by Bernard Crossland
Computer typeset by Peter Peregrinus Ltd.
Printed in Great Britain
by T. & A. Constable Ltd., Edinburgh

Clio Press Ltd.,
Woodside House, Hinksey Hill,
Oxford OX1 5BE, England.
Providing the services of the European
Bibliographical Centre and the American
Bibliographical Center.

American Bibliographical Center-Clio Press,
Riviera Campus, 2040 Alameda Padre Serra,
Santa Barbara, Ca. 93103, U.S.A.

*To my wife and son
whose contribution is unsung
but immeasurable*

Contents

Contents

Contents

Introduction

The land and the people

The early history of the area now known as Saudi Arabia is one of small pockets of settlement dependent upon trade surrounded by territory which was the province of the nomad, whose livelihood was derived mainly from camel breeding and raiding. Various small federations of city states held sway during the period up to the 6th century A.D., and Southern Arabia came into contact with the Persian and Roman empires as a trading station between East and West, but did not fall within the province of these empires.

Succeeding years saw little change in the pattern, and the interior was always immune from any change. Even the advent of Muhammad and the spread of Islam proved to be only a temporary unifying factor, for the successors of the Prophet could not exercise the same authority and old rivalries came to the surface again.

The beginnings of the present political pattern can be discerned in the important period which saw Ottoman control of the Arab world. This period began in the 16th century, although for Arabia control was only nominal. Even in the Hedjaz, it was never very strong, although the area did remain a province of the empire until World War I, as did 'Asir in the south. The influence of the Ottomans was exercised indirectly rather than through close control from Istanbul; they relied on internal rivalry as the means by which to divide and rule.

The Nejd in the centre of Arabia was largely untouched by events elsewhere, while the Gulf became a British sphere of influence and Yemen and Oman became virtually independent. However, the Nejd was the centre of a more important upheaval which drew inspiration from the original teachings of the Prophet. This reforming movement, known as the Wahhabi movement, became influential towards the end of the 18th century, and by 1800 its followers had taken Karbela and Najaf in Iraq, Damascus in Syria and Mecca and Medina in the Hedjaz. The triumph was short-lived as, at the behest of the Sultan, the forces of Muhammad Ali of Egypt defeated the Wahhabis during the period 1811–18 and finally in 1838.

Defeat did not, however, mean the end of the movement, and the Wahhabis, in alliance with the House of Saud, continued to rule the interior of the Nejd. The greatest threat to the movement and the House of Saud came towards the end of the 19th century from the tribe of Ibn Rashid of Hail, who had the support of the Turks. The immediate future for Ibn Saud was bleak and he was forced to flee, leaving his tribe to be ruled by the Rashids. In 1902 he returned from exile and with a small band of followers retook Riyadh; following this he defeated a combined Turkish-Rashidi force in 1904. A larger Turkish expedition succeeded in enforcing a presence in the al-Qasim district of the Nejd, but this only lasted until 1906, owing to the high desertion rate and the high rate of fatalities caused by disease among the Turkish troops. The family of Saud were now in complete control and in 1910, to preserve the ideals of the Wahhabi movement, the Ikhwan were established and settled in colonies throughout the Nejd; this formed the basis of a centralized organization to secure Saudi rule.

The entry of Turkey into World War I as an ally of Germany saw Arabia become a centre of political intrigue before there was any serious military activity. The details of the intrigues are too complex to discuss here, but basically the result was that the Gulf states, under British influence, severed their ties with Turkey, and Sherif Hussein of the Hedjaz entered into secret talks with Britain with a view to entering the war on the side of the Allies. However, the Turks were still present in the Hedjaz and 'Asir and had the continuing support of Ibn Rashid.

The future of the Nejd became inextricably drawn into the web of political intrigue which was being woven in the Middle East by the Great Powers and, indeed, by different departments of the British government. Division as to the policy to be followed centred on the desire of the India Office to support the aspirations of Ibn Saud, without any Arab revolt, while the Arab Bureau in Cairo favoured support for Hussein and an Arab revolt. The situation was further complicated by the tensions between Husssein and Ibn Saud, which were a threat to any policy adopted by Britain.

After protracted negotiations with Hussein an Arab revolt was declared on 5 June 1916; this meant that the policies of the Arab Bureau were to prevail throughout the war and during the subsequent peace negotiations. A subsidy was paid to Ibn Saud during this period to preserve his neutrality and to prevent any outbreak of hostilities between the Hedjaz and the Nejd. The success of the

Allies in the war and the intrigues at the peace talks still saw the Nejd in isolation, but at the same time Hussein's star was waning. He played an ineffectual role in the peace settlement and his unreasonable demands and self-aggrandizement eventually cost him the support of the British government.

Nevertheless, Hussein was rash enough to escalate the dispute with Ibn Saud by reviving territorial disputes which had lain dormant during the war. The situation was now different, for Ibn Saud, having disposed of Ibn Rashid, had grown in stature; his right to Shammar Hail and Jawf was recognized by the Indian government. Relations gradually deteriorated and the situation came to a climax in March 1924, when Hussein claimed the title of Caliph, thus arousing the wrath of the Ikhwan. Hussein's claim was not recognized by anyone and Ibn Saud declared him a traitor to Islam and an unfit protector of the holy places. The Ikhwan invaded the Hedjaz and resistance was quelled in months although Ali, Hussein's eldest son, succeeded in holding Jeddah until 1925. On 8 January 1926 Ibn Saud proclaimed himself King of the Hedjaz and paved the way for the creation of the kingdom of Saudi Arabia.

The changed situation was officially recognized by Britain in the Treaty of Jeddah in 1927; Ibn Saud agreed in turn to recognize Abdullah's rule in Transjordan, Faisal as ruler of Iraq, and Britain's presence in the Gulf. It had already been agreed in 1925 that the northern boundary of his territory would be limited by the mandate boundaries, while that in the south was settled in 1934 after protracted negotiations with Yemen and a brief war.

The primary task of Ibn Saud was to consolidate his position by trying to unify and develop his country; he pursued a policy of colonization based on the conception of the Ikhwan and the curbing of lawlessness amongst the Bedouin. A start was also made on improving the administration of the country, and on economic changes to counter the falling revenues from the Hajj, which represented the bulk of the country's revenue. The situation was resolved by the discovery of oil in Bahrain in 1932; this led to prospecting on the mainland and the beginning of a new era for Saudi Arabia.

Introduction

The bibliography

This bibliography makes no claim to completeness, but the material listed should provide a comprehensive picture of Saudi Arabia for the general reader, the librarian or the researcher. Arrangement is by broad subject heading and within that breakdown alphabetical by author or title. Cross-references have been used where necessary to refer the user back to the main entry which carries the annotation. As is the case with all bibliographers, my aim has been objectivity, but inevitably a subjective element is present. The annotations reflect my views when they are evaluative, and are provided in order to illustrate the content of the material. A few entries are not annotated; this is not a reflection on their value but represents an assessment, on my part, that it was not essential. As a deliberate policy all general trade and national bibliographies have been excluded and only English-language or translated items have been listed. The early history of the Arabian Peninsula has also been excluded, as a means of keeping the work within manageable bounds and a reflection of likely usage. The section on oil has also been kept brief, as detailed treatment would merit a separate bibliography. I cannot recommend too highly the use of the other bibliographies listed in the section devoted to them, and the general reference books, in particular the various Middle East yearbooks and the *Index Islamicus.*

The Country and its People

General works on Saudi Arabia

1 Saudi Arabia: beyond the sands of Mecca.
Thomas J. Abercrombie. *National Geographic*, vol. 129, pt. 1
(Jan. 1966), p. 1-53. map.
The author of the article is a Moslem and, as a guest of the Saudi Arabian govern-
ment, was able to visit the holy places. This is a useful survey of the country and its
development and is well illustrated by coloured photographs taken by the author.

2 Aramco handbook: oil and the Middle East.
Arabian American Oil Company. Dhahran, Saudi Arabia:
Aramco, 1968. 279p.
A beautifully illustrated book on Saudi Arabia which covers history, the oil industry
and Aramco in particular, statistical information, and the culture and customs of the
people.

3 Miracle of the desert kingdom.
Ahmad Assah. London: Johnson, 1969. 330p. maps.
A comprehensive study of Saudi Arabia dealing with the historical background, both
past and contemporary. Also considered in detail is the role of Faisal in the development of Saudi Arabia, and his form of administration and style of government. The
author also deals with oil policies, economic development plans, and questions of
finance, educational programmes, and social change.

The Country and its People. General works on Saudi Arabia

4 A handbook of Arabia.
Great Britain. Admiralty. Naval Intelligence Division.   London:
H.M. Stationery Office, 1917. 709p. maps. (Geographical
Handbook Series).

Although dated this is still a useful reference source. The series was designed to provide material for an understanding of the political problems in countries with a British interest. As such the handbooks cover all aspects, with each section compiled by a specialist, and they are well supported by plates and maps.

5 Western Arabia and the Red Sea.
Great Britain. Admiralty. Naval Intelligence Division.   London:
H.M. Stationery Office, 1946. 659p. maps. (Geographical
Handbook Series).

The same comments apply as to the previous item. The main sections are: 1. Introductory; 2. Geology and physical geography; 3. Coastal regions; 4. Climate and vegetation; 5. History; 6. Administration; 7. The people; 8. Public health and disease; 9. Agriculture; 10. Economic geography; 11. Ports and towns.

6 Saudi Arabia.
Great Britain. Dept. of Trade and Industry. British Overseas Trade
Board.   London: H.M. Stationery Office, regularly revised. 48p.
maps. (Hints to Businessmen Series).

A useful publication giving basic information, useful addresses, and hints on living conditions, etc., of value to the traveller and businessman.

7 Saudi Arabia.
John S. Haupert.   *Focus* (New York), vol. 16, pt. 4 (1966), p.
1-6. map.

A survey article on Saudi Arabia providing background information at an introductory level. The article is divided into the following subject areas: 1. Physical geography; 2. Climate; 3. Agriculture and settlement; 4. Transport; 5. Foreign trade and economic development.

8 Saudi Arabia.
John S. Haupert.   In: *The Middle East*, edited by Alice Taylor.
Newton Abbot, England: David & Charles, 1972, p. 99-111.

This contribution deals with various aspects of Saudi Arabia, the deserts, agriculture and settlement, oil and industry, transport and communications, foreign trade and economic development, education, and town planning.

9 Saudi Arabia.
Edited by David Hinnawi.   *Arab World*, vol. 11, pt. 3 (1965), p.
84-90.

A general survey of Saudi Arabia and developments in its economy.

10 Saudi Arabia today: introduction to the richest oil power.
Peter Hobday.   London: Macmillan, 1978. 144p. map.

A consideration of the challenge faced by Saudi Arabia, particularly in the field of economic and social development. Also examined are the position and role of the Saudi royal family, and the role of the country in world affairs.

11 The kingdom of Saudi Arabia.
London: Stacey International, 1977. 256p. maps. bibliog.

The work is compiled by a series of contributors and is lavishly illustrated with coloured plates and maps. It is a useful introduction to the country and a basic reference guide when used with other more detailed works. The 11 major sections are: 1. The country; 2. The cities; 3. The people, their habitat - way of life; 4. History; 5. Islam; 6. Culture; 7. Government; 8. Industry - development; 9. Youth; 10. Social development; 11. The future.

12 The Arabia of Ibn Saud.
Ray Leblicker (and others).   New York: Russell Moore, 1952. 179p.

A well-illustrated book and the forerunner of the *Aramco handbook*. It deals briefly with the geography and history of Saudi Arabia and its culture.

13 Come along to Saudi Arabia.
L. Edmond Leipold.   Minneapolis, Minnesota: Denison, 1974. 167p. maps.

Designed as an introduction to the kingdom.

14 Saudi Arabia: its people, its society, its culture.
George A. Lipsky (and others).   New Haven, Connecticut: Human Relations Area Files Press, 1959. 366p. (Survey of World Cultures Series).

Although somewhat dated this is still a very useful introductory work.

15 Saudi Arabia.
David E. Long.   Beverly Hills, California; London: Sage Publications for the Centre for Strategic and International Studies, Georgetown University, 1976. 71p. map. bibliog. (Washington Papers, no. 39).

A very valuable guide to Saudi Arabia, giving an account of its historical development, an overview of the economy, the political and administrative process, and a future projection especially emphasizing the field of foreign relations. Genealogical tables are included.

16 Research in Saudi Arabia.
C. D. Mathews.   *Muslim World*, vol. 43, pt. 2 (1954), p. 110-25.

An article on the research programme of Aramco, not strictly related to the technical side of the operation. Aspects considered are mapping activities, toponymic studies,

The Country and its People. General works on Saudi Arabia

the history of Eastern Arabia, linguistic studies, and the production of educational films on topics such as water conservation, and health and hygiene.

17 Finding one's feet in Saudi Arabia.
Trevor Mostyn. *Middle East International*, no. 60 (June 1976), p. 27-8.
Examines the conditions faced by expatriate employees in Saudi Arabia, concentrating on the problems of social conditions, especially those resulting from the Wahhabi influence.

18 The green book: guide for living in Saudi Arabia.
Margaret Pendleton, and others. Washington, D.C.: Middle East Editorial Associates, 1976. 118p. bibliog.
An attempt to deal with the everyday problems faced by expatriates living and working in Saudi Arabia, pointing the way in a positive manner to living with the difficulties. The authors also provide a background sketch to various aspects of the kingdom.

19 The businessman's guide to Saudi Arabia.
Edited by Alan Purdy. London: Arlington Books, 1976. 130p. maps.

20 A sketch of the geography, people and history of the Arabian peninsula.
G. Rentz. Dhahran, Saudi Arabia: Aramco, 1960, 67p.
Designed as an introduction to Saudi Arabia for employees of the company.

21 Background notes: Saudi Arabia.
United States. Department of State. Washington, D.C.: Department of State, 1965. 4p.
Some basic introductory information on the country.

22 Business directory of Saudi Arabia.
University Securities Ltd. Business Aids Division. London: The Division, 1974; New York: British Book Center, 1976. 143p. maps.

23 Area handbook for Saudi Arabia.
Norman C. Walpole (and others). Washington, D.C.: U.S. Government Printing Office, 1971. 373p. maps. bibliog. (Foreign Area Studies).
A guide to Saudi Arabia giving basic facts about social, economic, political and military institutions.

Saudi Arabia in general works on the Middle East

24 The Middle East: a handbook.
Edited by Michael Adams. London: Blond; New York: Praeger, 1971. 633p. maps. bibliog.

Although dated, still a very useful work, although the first section's comparative statistics and country by country facts and figures must be handled carefully because of the book's age. The second part of the work presents surveys on the countries of the area, and that on Saudi Arabia, by Edmond Y. Asfour on p. 271-81, provides a good introduction for both the general reader and the serious student, covering the historical background, political developments to World War I, internal consolidation, World War II and the postwar years, constitution and government, economic growth, and social development. The chapter on oil, p. 427-41, by W. W. Stewart, deals with the historical background and development of the industry and then with the individual oil-producing countries, and concludes with a consideration of the role of oil in the economy of the Middle East, and its future prospects. The essay on natural resources and economic structure and growth in the Middle East covers the resources available, their significance, and the relevant statistics. Also covered is the technological change in the area, brought about largely by the technical aspects of the oil industry. The chapter on agriculture, p. 415-26, by H. Bowen-Jones, treats Saudi Arabia in a limited way, while on p. 485-92 there is a short study of Islamic society and its structure. Education is covered on p. 504-15, and the treatment includes a general overview, the question of female education, the various levels of education, and adult education and literacy. Literature and art in the Middle East are dealt with under the headings 'Arab literature', p. 535-42; 'Art in the Arab states of the Middle East', p. 563-72; and 'Arabic music', p. 580-3. On p. 584-98 there is discussion of the press, the pattern of mass media systems, the growth of broadcasting and films, and the control of the mass media.

25 Annual register of world events. Section V. The Middle East and North Africa.
London: Longman; New York: St. Martin's Press, annual.

An account of the significant events in Saudi Arabia and other countries of the Arab world, produced annually.

26 The Arab world today.
Morroe Berger. London: Weidenfeld & Nicolson; Garden City, New York: Doubleday, 1962. 480p. maps. bibliog.

Although Saudi Arabia is only briefly dealt with in this work, the book is of interest as a study of the contemporary Arab world, showing the interrelationship of religious, geographic, historical, economic, and political factors.

27 The Arabs: their history and future.
Jacques Berque. London: Faber, 1964. 310p.

A useful background work.

28 Beyond the veil of Arabia.
J. Bisch, translated by Reginald Spink. London: Allen & Unwin, 1962. 148p. map.

A useful introductory book for the general reader.

29 Major companies of the Arab world.
Edited by G. Bricault. London: Graham & Trotman, 1977. 559p.

A directory aimed at the businessman.

30 The Middle East: a political and economic survey.
Edited by R. Bullard. London: Royal Institute for International Affairs, 1961. 3rd ed. 569p. maps.

An extremely good survey representing a British interpretation of the situation.

31 March arabesque.
Emile Bustani. London: Hale, 1961. 216p. maps.

A general history of the Arab world, much of it relevant to Saudi Arabia. This is the type of work which, although wide in context, is useful not only for information on Saudi Arabia, but also for placing the country in the context of the area. Chapter 10 includes discussion of the Ibn Saud-Hussein rivalry and the creation of Saudi Arabia.

32 Common sense about the Arab world.
Erskine Childers. London: Gollancz, 1960. 192p.

A general survey of the Arab world providing the general reader with an insight into the region. No index.

33 Crossroads: land and life in Southwest Asia.
George Babcock Cressey. London: Pitman; Philadelphia, Pennsylvania: Lippincott, 1960. 593p. maps.

A useful introduction to the culture and society of the area.

34 Heritage of the desert: the Arabs and the Middle East.
Harry B. Ellis. New York: Roland Press, 1956. 311p. maps. bibliog.

The author was Middle East correspondent for the *Christian Science Monitor*, and the value of this book lies in its evaluation of the Arab peoples.

35 The crescent in crisis: an interpretive study of the modern Arab world.
Nabih Amin Faris, Mohammed Husayne. Lawrence, Kansas: University of Kansas Press, 1955. 191p.

A valuable work which deals with the Arab world as a national unit, looking at the unifying factors and those which have worked against unity. The unifying factors are of two types: those that are basic such as language, history, religion, and mentality;

and the new factors such as education, communications, the media, and economic development.

36 **The Middle East: a history.**

Sydney Nettleton Fisher.   Westminster, Maryland: Knopf, 1968; London: Routledge & Kegan Paul, 1971. 2nd ed. 749p. maps. bibliog.

Although much of the earlier part of this work, such as the geographic background and the early history, is of relevance, the main section on Saudi Arabia is Chapter 38 entitled 'Oil and Arabia'. This chapter traces the rise of Ibn Saud, from the conflict with Hussein, and the creation of Saudi Arabia. Discussion then centres upon the discovery of oil and the effect this had on the Saudi economy and the resultant social change. Also considered is the growth of Saudi military power in the Arab world, and her relations with her Middle East neighbours.

37 **The Middle East: a physical, social and regional geography.**

William B. Fisher.   London: Methuen; Scranton, Pennsylvania: Barnes & Noble, 1971. 6th ed. 571p. maps.

A good introductory work mainly aimed at the student, but valuable as a starting point for more detailed studies.

38 **Empire by treaty: Britain and the Middle East in the twentieth century.**

Matthew A. Fitzsimons.   Scranton, Pennsylvania: University of Notre Dame Press, 1964. (International Studies Series); London: Benn, 1965. 235p. map.

This work is devoted to an examination of British policies in the Middle East which the author considers benefited Britain and the Middle East countries concerned. Saudi Arabia is briefly mentioned, mainly in connection with the Arab League, the Baghdad Pact, and other areas of British involvement in the affairs of the Middle East.

39 **The Arabs.**

H. A. R. Gibb.   London, New York: Oxford University Press, 1940. 32p. maps. (Oxford Pamphlets on World Affairs, no. 40).

A consideration of the Arab world in general terms, dealing with its background and history, the impact of the West, and the re-awakening of Arab consciousness.

40 **Iraq and the Persian Gulf.**

Great Britain. Admiralty. Naval Intelligence Division.   London: Admiralty, Naval Intelligence Division, 1944. 682p. maps. (Geographical Handbook Series).

One of a series of handbooks, compiled by the geographical section of the Naval Intelligence Division, designed to provide material for the discussion of naval, military and political problems. A great deal of this volume is outside the scope of this study by virtue of geography, but the Persian Gulf section is of particular value for a study of Saudi Arabia's eastern province.

The Country and its People
Saudi Arabia in general works on the Middle East

41 Gulf handbook.
London: Trade & Travel Publications, annual.

The country surveys are the main feature of this work, and these are of a very high standard. The background aspects necessary for an understanding of Saudi Arabia are given, beginning with its history, geography, economy, agriculture, etc. Also included is a 'Diary of main events' which gives some indication of the previous twelve months' significant developments. The remainder of the survey is concerned with statistics, general information of value to the visitor, and details of the newspapers and periodicals of the area. Of particular value are the indexes to advertisers by name and trade classification, as well as an index to place-names. The work is well illustrated with political maps and maps of the major centres. This provides a welcome addition to a quick-reference collection on the Arab world and Saudi Arabia.

42 Seas of sand.
Paul Hamilton. London: Aldus Books, 1971. 191p. maps. (Aldus Encyclopaedia of Discovery and Exploration).

Not all of this work is relevant by nature of geography, but a great deal of it is concerned with early exploration, visits to Mecca and Medina, the exploration of the Nejd, and the empty quarter. The book is well illustrated and a useful introduction for the general reader.

43 History of the Arabs.
Philip K. Hitti. London: Macmillan; New York: St. Martin's Press, 1970. 10th ed. 767p. maps.

Although this volume covers a wider area than Saudi Arabia, it is an extremely valuable and readable account for both the general reader and the specialist.

44 The Arabs: a short history.
Philip K. Hitti. London: Macmillan, 1968. 4th ed. 224p. maps; Chicago, Illinois: Henry Regnery, 1956.

An abbreviated version of the previous item.

45 The Middle East: problem area in world politics.
Halford L. Hoskins. New York: Macmillan, 1957. 311p. maps.

A general examination of the place of the Middle East in world affairs, in which Saudi Arabia is briefly mentioned, particularly in relation to oil and the Arab League.

46 The Arabs.
Arnold Hottinger. London: Thames & Hudson, 1963. 344p. maps.

A general examination of the culture, history, and place of the Arabs in the modern world. Saudi Arabia is only dealt with briefly, mainly in connection with the rise of the Wahhabi movement and the rivalry between Hussein and Ibn Saud.

47 Political trends in the Arab world: the role of ideas and ideals in politics.

Majid Khadduri. London; Baltimore, Maryland: Johns Hopkins Press, 1970. 298p.

This study is concerned with political trends in the Arab world, and with the question of Islam in the Arab world and its role in a changing Arab society.

48 Nationalism and imperialism in the Hither East.

Hans Kohn. London: Routledge; New York: Howard Fertig, 1932. 339p.

This book is valuable as a study of political and nationalistic developments in the Middle East, though it is mainly concerned with areas other than Saudi Arabia.

49 The emergence of the modern Middle East: selected readings.

Compiled by Robert Geron Landen. Cincinnati, Ohio: Van Nostrand Reinhold, 1970; London: Van Nostrand Reinhold, 1971. 366p.

A selection of primary source material designed to show the modernization of the Middle East from the 19th century onwards.

50 The Middle East in world affairs.

George Lenczowski. Ithaca, New York: Cornell University Press, 1962. 3rd ed. 576p. maps. bibliog.

In this detailed work the first section of three chapters is of general interest as it deals with the historical background prior to the First World War, the war in the Middle East, and the peace settlement. Saudi Arabia as a separate entity is dealt with in Chapter 12, p. 431-54, beginning with the power and prestige of Ibn Saud, the discovery of oil, the Second World War, Saudi-American friendship, and internal and foreign developments in the 1950s. Saudi Arabia is also discussed in Chapter 16, p. 501-16, in connection with the founding and activities of the Arab League.

51 Encyclopaedia of Islam.

Edited by B. Lewis, J. Schacht. Leiden: Brill; Atlantic Highlands, New Jersey: Humanities Press, 1953- , in progress. New ed.

Indispensable for any study of the Middle East, with many relevant articles, each contributed by an expert. Particularly valuable for a study of the early Wahhabi movement and the establishment of the Ikhwan.

52 The Middle East: a social geography.

S. H. Longrigg, J. Jankowski. London: Duckworth, 1970. 2nd rev. ed. 291p. maps. bibliog.

In addition to the specific section on Saudi Arabia (p. 154-9), which gives a condensed geographical picture, references can be found throughout the text dealing with various aspects of society and geography.

53 **Gazetteer of the Persian Gulf, Oman and Saudi Arabia.**
John G. Lorimer. Calcutta, India: Government Printing House,
1908. 2 vols.; Reprinted, Farnborough, England: Gregg
International, 1970; Dublin: Irish Academic Press, 1970; Totowa,
New Jersey: Irish Academic Press, 1971.
Indispensable for the study of Anglo-Wahhabi relations and of the growth of British
interests in the Gulf region.

54 **The Arabs.**
Peter Mansfield. London: Allen Lane, 1976. 572p. map.
A major contribution to the study of the social, political and historical aspects of the
Arab world, including Saudi Arabia which is dealt with specifically on p. 400-9. The
first part of the book deals with the historical aspects of the subject, including the
Wahhabi movement, the Arab position during the First World War, and the rivalry
between Hussein and Ibn Saud. The second section is a country by country survey as
indicated above, but Saudi Arabia is also dealt with in connection with relations with
Egypt, the Yemen civil war, and the border disputes with Kuwait, Oman and the
United Arab Emirates. The final section deals with the contemporary Arab world,
considering the revival of Arab fortunes, the question of Palestine, the hopes for Arab
unity, and the power resulting from the position of oil in the world economy.

55 **The Middle East: a political and economic survey.**
Edited by Peter Mansfield. London, New York: Oxford
University Press, 1973. 4th ed. 591p. map. bibliog.
An important work divided into three main sections, the first introductory, the second
consisting of thematic studies, and the third a country by country survey. The
introductory section is a useful starting point as it defines the region, gives a historical
and political outline, deals with the religious question, and contains a brief economic
and social survey. The country section on Saudi Arabia (p. 136-53) deals briefly with
all aspects of the country: its history, geography, society, agriculture, oil industry, and
transport system.

56 **The Middle East and North Africa.**
London: Europa Publications, annual.
The standard reference tool, and for many years the only one available. It is divided
into four parts, the first being a general survey containing articles on various aspects
of the Middle East. The second section deals with the work of organizations in the
area, including the various operations of the United Nations and other bodies. The
third deals exclusively with the various countries, broken down into physical and
social geography, history, the economy, a statistical section, a directory, and a short
bibliography. The last section covers other reference material; a brief biographical
section; details concerning calendars and weights and measures; research bodies; and a
listing of general bibliographies.

57 **Middle East yearbook.**
London: Middle East Magazine Ltd., annual.
This is a completely new reference work which first appeared in 1977. It is prepared
by the Centre for Middle Eastern and Islamic Studies at the University of Durham.
The publication is in four sections covering various background features, the position
of the Middle East in relation to the rest of the world, its economy, and a country by
country survey. The country survey comprises the bulk of the volume and is prefaced

by an introductory article giving brief details on the history, economy, etc. Potted facts are then given concerning geography, climate, population, educational facilities, public services, etc., and statistical data on production, oil statistics, and budget information. The value of the work is enhanced by numerous maps covering oil production and refining, agriculture, population, etc. Also of value are the various specialist articles dealing with concepts such as construction programmes, development plans, etc.

58 Middle East perspective.
R. C. Mowat. London: Blandford, 1958. 279p. maps. bibliog.

Attempts to provide a perspective of the area in world affairs, at a time of renewed interest, due to significant events in the region.

59 The Arabs: a narrative history from Mohammed to the present.
Anthony Nutting. London: Hollis & Carter, 1964; London, New York: New American Library, 1967. 424p. maps. bibliog.

A general history of the Arab peoples from the beginnings of the Arab empire. In view of its coverage great detail is not possible, but this is a very readable account providing a useful introduction.

60 The Middle East today.
D. Peretz. London, New York: Holt, Rinehart & Winston, 1963. 2nd ed., 1971. 483p. maps.

Good general coverage of the area and its growing economic significance.

61 Colours of the Arab fatherland.
Angelo Pesce. London, New York: Oleander Press, 1976. 2nd ed. 144p. (Arabia Past and Present Series, no. 1).

An interesting introduction to the history and traditions of Saudi Arabia.

62 The changing patterns of the Middle East, 1919-1958.
Pierre Rondot. London: Chatto & Windus, 1961. 221p.

The author deals with the transition of the Middle East during the period in question, and as such Saudi Arabia is referred to frequently throughout the text, mainly in connection with relations between Saudi Arabia and Egypt.

63 The Arab world, Inc.
John J. Putman. *National Geographic*, vol. 148, pt. 4 (Oct. 1975), p. 494-533. map.

An account of the oil-producing states and the development programmes being financed by oil revenues. Apart from the introductory section, Saudi Arabia is considered on p. 518-22.

The Country and its People
Saudi Arabia in general works on the Middle East

64 The Arabian peninsula.
Richard H. Sanger. Ithaca, New York: Cornell University Press, 1954. 295p. maps. bibliog. Reprinted, Plainview, New York: Books for Libraries.

A survey covering the states of the Arabian peninsula as a whole, based partly on personal experience, and partly on official accounts from the United States Department of State. The book concentrates mainly on changes brought about by Western influences in the area, and particularly on the role of the United States.

65 Britain and the Arab states: a survey of Anglo-Arab relations, 1920-1948.
M. V. Seton-Williams. London: Luzac, 1948. 330p. maps.

A useful handbook for the study of contemporary relations between Great Britain and the Arab states, supplemented by documents and maps.

66 The Middle East: temple of Janus.
Desmond Stewart. London: Hamish Hamilton, 1972. 414p. bibliog.

A well-written general history of the Middle East, and a valuable introduction to any study of the area as a whole.

67 The Arab world.
Edited by D. Stewart. New York: Time-Life International, 1962. 160p.

A well-illustrated introduction to the area.

68 The Middle East.
Edited by Alice Taylor. Newton Abbot, England: David & Charles, 1972. 223p. maps.

This work is divided into two parts, the first being an overview of the region as a whole, whilst the second part is a country by country survey, with that devoted to Saudi Arabia on p. 99-111. Of particular interest in the first part are the following: 'The challenge of change: petroleum and planning' by J. A. Bill, p. 9-16; 'Cities of the Middle East' by R. S. Harrison, p. 17-26; 'The desert and the sown: an ecological appraisal' by J. R. Manners, p. 27-37.

69 The Arab experience.
Antony Thomas, Michael Deakin, Robin Constable. London: Namara Publications, 1975. 175p.

This book was a by-product of research for a documentary television series of the same name. It is well illustrated with photographs by Robin Constable. It includes a useful introductory outline (p. 105-54), which attempts to 'entertain and inform anyone who has ever wanted to penetrate the mysterious East', and 'who wishes to grasp the pleasure and importance of the Arab experience'.

70 **Modernisation of the Arab world.**
Edited by Jack Howell Thompson, R. D. Reischauer.   London,
New York: Van Nostrand, 1966. 249p.
A useful general account of changes in the Middle East, including Saudi Arabia.

71 **Arabian peninsula, official standard names approved by the Board.**
United States Board on Geographical Names.   Washington,
D.C.: Office of Geography, Department of the Interior, 1961.
458p.
An extremely important work guiding the student or researcher through a difficult area of study.

72 **The kingdom of oil: the Middle East, its people and its power.**
Ray Vicker.   New York: Scribner, 1974; London: Hale, 1975.
264p.
This work deals with the Middle East country by country (Saudi Arabia on p. 98-122), and attempts to portray to the interested reader the oil-producing countries and the part they play in world affairs.

73 **The Near East: a modern history.**
William Yale.   Ann Arbor, Michigan: University of Michigan
Press, 1958. Rev. ed. 1968. 485p.
A general history of the area with extensive references to Saudi Arabia: V. Foreign affairs and domestic crisis, p. 62-81, deals with the Wahhabi movement and the intervention of Muhammad Ali. XIII. The Arab renaissance and nationalist movement 1866-1914, p. 187-203. XVII. The Arab revolt, p. 250-61. XXIII. Arabia, p. 351-63, gives a geographical and historical outline of Saudi Arabia, including demography and cultural change. XXIV. Oil in the Near and Middle East, p. 364-79. XXVI. Arab Near East during World War II, p. 398-413, considers the strategic importance of Saudi Arabia.

Exploration and Travel

General

74 **Travellers in Arabia.**
Robin L. Bidwell. London: Hamlyn, 1976. 224p. maps.
bibliog.
This work brings together the major explorations of Arabia, the latter part dealing with
Oman and the Yemen. Major travellers such as Burton, Palgrave, Doughty, and
Philby, are dealt with in a readable and informative manner, providing a useful
introduction to the various explorations and the writings of the explorers themselves. A
useful introduction for the interested general reader, and a useful refresher for the
specialist.

75 **Far Arabia: explorers of the myth.**
Peter Brent. London: Weidenfeld & Nicolson, 1977. 239p.
maps.
This work discusses the image that the Western world has of Arabia, through the
accounts of the various explorers, which tended to create a legendary atmosphere that
was far removed from reality. This is an extremely readable account of exploration in
the area, from its earlier explorers through to Wilfred P. Thesiger.

76 **Dangerous guides: English writers and the desert.**
M. Foss. *New Middle East*, vol. 9 (1969), p. 38-42.
An article warning the reader of the dangers of uncritically accepting that early
accounts of travel in the Arabian peninsula present an accurate picture of the situation.

77 **Explorers of Arabia: from the Renaissance to the end of the
Victorian era.**
Zahra Freeth, H. Victor F. Winstone. London: Allen & Unwin,
1978. 308p. maps.
A collection of extracts designed to illustrate the work of nine explorers of Arabia: 1.
Lodovico Varthema; 2. Joseph Pitts; 3. Carsten Niebuhr; 4. Jean Louis Burckhardt; 5.

Richard Burton; 6. William Gifford Palgrave; 7. Carlo Guarmani; 8. Charles M. Doughty; 9. The Blunts.

78 **The unveiling of Arabia: the story of Arabian travel and discovery.**
Reginald H. Kiernan.   London: Harrap, 1937. 359p. maps.

A survey of Western exploration in the Arabian peninsula, containing extracts from the travellers' own accounts. Although more comprehensive than Hogarth's account by virtue of date, that by Hogarth is better for the explorations described in both books.

79 **The Arabs and the English.**
Sani J. Nasir.   London: Longman, 1976. 192p. bibliog.

The author has undertaken an examination of the stereotypes of the Arabs, as they are seen in the West, mainly through the accounts of various travellers. It is important to understand the effects of the information provided by these accounts, as they have coloured contemporary views, especially with regard to Arab society and culture. The two chapters dealing with the exploration of the peninsula are particularly relevant. The first deals with 19th century explorers such as Burton, Blunt, Doughty, Palgrave, and Hogarth, and the romantic image of the peninsula portrayed by the travellers. The second relevant section is entitled 'Image in flux' and deals with 20th century explorers and soldiers such as Lawrence, St. John Philby, and Glubb. This section also deals with the effects of newspapers and radio on the image and, in particular, the image as portrayed by the cinema.

Exploration and travel before 1900

80 **Some early travellers in Arabia.**
C. F. Beckingham.   *Journal of the Royal Asiatic Society,* vol. 48, pt. 3-4 (1949), p. 155-76.

This article deals with journeys made, or alleged to have been made, during the period between the middle of the 15th and the middle of the 17th century. Not all of these journeys are documented in the standard works on the early exploration of Arabia, owing to the little use made of Portuguese historians. This article seeks to rectify these omissions.

81 **A pilgrimage to Nejd, the cradle of the Arab race, a visit to the court of the Arab Emir and our Persian campaign.**
Lady Anne Blunt.   London: John Murray, 1881. 2 vols. maps. Reprinted, London: Cass; Forest Grove, Oregon: International Scholarly Book Services, 1968.

One of the classic (illustrated) accounts of exploration of Arabia. Includes genealogical tables.

Exploration and Travel. Exploration and travel before 1900

82 **Doughty's mirror of Arabia.**
M. Brittain. *Muslim World*, vol. 37, pt. 1 (1947), p. 42-8.
A critique of Charles M. Doughty's *Travels in Arabia deserta* which assesses the book itself and its significance for a greater understanding of the Arab world. In view of the unique place occupied by Doughty's book in the literature of Arabia, such a critique is useful in helping to put it in perspective.

83 **Travels in Arabia: comprehending an account of those territories in Hedjaz which the Mohammedans regard as sacred.**
John Lewis Burckhardt. London: Colburn, 1829. 478p. maps. Reprinted, London: Cass; Forest Grove, Oregon: International Scholarly Book Services, 1968.
Another classic account of 19th century travel in Arabia.

84 **Personal narrative of a pilgrimage to el Madinah and Meccah.**
Sir Richard F. Burton. London: Longman, 1855. 3 vols. maps.
The classic account of the major Victorian explorer who maintained that he visited the holy places in disguise.

85 **Travels in Arabia deserta.**
Charles M. Doughty. London: Cape, 1926. 690p. maps.
This is one of several editions of what has become a classic travel account and, indeed, in the preface to this edition T. E. Lawrence termed it 'a book not like other books, but something particular, a bible of its kind'. Doughty's journey was made in the 1870s, and he spent two years among the Bedouin of northern Arabia, living a similar life style, suffering robbery and deprivations, and openly admitting his Christian religion. As an account of everyday life in the area, it is without equal when combined with the detailed topographical and archaeological material and the descriptions of the flora and fauna. This is not an easy book to read and is really only of relevance to someone interested in the area requiring a detailed knowledge and a taste of 'the soul of the desert'. Also of relevance is the introduction by Lawrence which, while concerned with Doughty's work, is also a survey of development in Arabia during the fifty years after the book was first written.

86 **Wanderings in Arabia.**
Charles M. Doughty. London: Duckworth, 1949. 607p. maps.
An abridgement of *Arabia deserta*, done by Edward Garnett with the author's approval. This is an easier edition to read than the previous editions, concentrating mainly on the topographical and social history aspects of the exploration.

87 **George Forster Sadleir (1789-1859), first European to cross Arabia.**
F. M. Edwards. *Journal of the Royal Central Asian Society*, vol. 44, pt. 1 (1957), p. 38-49.

88 Arabia felix: the Danish expedition to Arabia of 1761-67.

Thorkild Hansen, translated by James McFarlane, Kathleen McFarlane. London: Collins, 1964. 381p. maps.

The first organized expedition to Arabia, largely forgotten in the light of subsequent exploration. A great deal of the book is concerned with the backgrounds of the members of the expedition, and the period spent in Egypt and Palestine. An interesting book if only because of the period of coverage.

89 The penetration of Arabia: a record of the development of Western knowledge concerning the Arabian peninsula.

David George Hogarth. London: Alston Rivers, 1905. 359p.

An account of the exploration of Arabia from earliest times. This book is very well written, well illustrated, and has become a classic.

90 Pioneer in Arabia.

David Mitchell. *Middle East International*, no. 62 (Aug. 1976), p. 26-8.

A brief account of a journey across the Arabian peninsula by George Forster Sadleir in the 1820s, of which little information remains except for a rare printing of his diary and reports, issued in 1866 at Bombay. Although the journey was political, being inspired by the Indian Government's desire to make an alliance with Ibrahim Pasha following his defeat of the Wahhabis, the trip was only of interest historically and geographically.

91 Sir Richard Burton.

Arthur Orrmont. London: Watts, 1972. 188p. maps. bibliog.

A life of Burton, aimed at the general reader, but a useful introduction to his exploration of Arabia.

92 Narrative of a year's journey through central and eastern Arabia: 1862-63.

William Gifford Palgrave. London: Macmillan, 1865. 2 vols. Reprinted, Farnborough, England: Gregg International, 1969.

One of the classic accounts of early exploration in Arabia.

93 Report on a journey to Riyadh in central Arabia.

Sir Lewis Pelly. Bombay: Government Press, 1866. 100p. map. Reprinted, London, New York: Oleander Press, 1978.

An account of a journey made in 1865 to investigate the Wahhabi influence in Arabia as a political force.

94 Riyadh: ancient and modern.

H. St. John B. Philby. *Middle East Journal*, vol. 13, pt. 2 (1959), p. 129-41.

The article discusses the visit of Palgrave to Riyadh in the 19th century, and updates the explorer's account by describing the modernization of the city by Ibn Saud.

95 A true and faithful account of the religion and manners of the Muhammadans.

Joseph Pitts. Exeter, England: Bishop & Stone, 1704.

The author was a British sailor captured and sold as a slave, who rose high in the household of his owner. Whilst a slave, Pitts undertook the pilgrimage to Mecca, with his owner, and his account gives an interesting picture of the difficulties faced on the Hajj at that time.

96 Desert city: an account of Hail in central Arabia.

J. M. Richards. *Architectural Review*, vol. 105 (1949), p. 35-41.

The photographs accompanying the article were taken in 1944 on an anti-locust expedition, aimed at eradicating the locust during a year in which food supplies in south-east Europe were expected to be critical. The majority of the text accompanying the photographs is taken from accounts of the early explorers such as G. A. Wallin and W. G. Palgrave.

97 Early Western cartography and the Arabian peninsula.

G. R. Tibbetts. *Malayan Journal of Tropical Geography*, vol. 3 (1954), p. 15-26.

An examination of how early cartographers saw the Arabian peninsula before any detailed exploration had been undertaken.

98 G. A. Wallin and the penetration of Arabia.

M. Trautz. *Geographical Journal*, vol. 76, pt. 3 (1930), p. 248-52.

This article attempts to put the explorations of Wallin in the Nejd into perspective, because of the paucity of material available in English. The journeys in question were made between 1845-46 and 1848.

99 A forgotten explorer of Arabia: G. A. Wallin.

M. Trautz. *Journal of the Royal Central Asian Society*, vol. 19, pt. 1 (1932), p. 131-50.

An interesting account of the explorations of G. A. Wallin, who was a native of Finland, but Swedish by blood and speech, and an explorer of the Arabian peninsula in the 1840s; he passed himself off as a Muslim, and practised medicine. The author feels that Wallin's exploratory work in Arabia places him high amongst Arabian explorers, and that his diaries and letters are worthy of greater study.

100 Travels in Arabia.

J. R. Wellsted. London, 1838. 2 vols. Reprinted, London: Cass, 1968.

Mainly concerned with the Sultanate of Oman, but the author did venture into the southwestern corner of Saudi Arabia.

Jiddah: portrait of an Arabian city.
See item no. 674.

20th century exploration and travel

101 [Notes and reports on Philby's mission].
Arab Bulletin, nos. 75, 78, 80, 81 (Jan.-March 1918).
A series of notes and reports on St. John Philby's mission to Ibn Saud, including an account of his journey across Arabia. At the time these were classified and were the main source of information, but they have now been superseded by Philby's postwar writings.

102 Kings and camels: an American in Saudi Arabia.
Grant C. Butler. New York: Devin-Adair, 1960. 206p.
A popular description of Saudi Arabia, its culture, economy and society. A useful introduction for the reader who knows nothing about the region.

103 Baghdad to Damascus via el Jauf, northern Arabia.
S. S. Butler. *Geographical Journal,* vol. 33, pt. 5 (1909), p. 517-35.
A journey to Damascus, approaching from the east and skirting the northern part of the Nejd, at a period when the Rashids were in control of the area.

104 Captain Shakespear's last journey.
Douglas Carruthers. *Geographical Journal,* vol. 59, pt. 5 (1922), p. 321-34; pt. 6, p. 401-18. maps.
A very detailed account of Shakespear's exploration of the Nejd in 1912, with extensive quotations from the explorer's own accounts.

105 Arabian journey, and other desert travels.
Gerald De Gaury. London: Harrap, 1950. 190p. maps.
The author was the first British minister to the court of Ibn Saud, and these accounts provide an interesting description of the social and economic life of Saudi Arabia, including problems that were beginning to show as a result of the changes taking place in the postwar period.

106 Arabia phoenix.
Gerald De Gaury. London: Harrap, 1946. 169p.
An interesting account of a visit to Saudi Arabia and a meeting with Ibn Saud, together with an account of the Wahhabi movement and its role in the development of the kingdom.

107 Saudi adventure.
Alistair Duncan. *Arab World,* vol. 26 (1970), p. 3-10.
An account of a tour of Saudi Arabia, made to cover in general all aspects of the country.

Exploration and Travel. 20th century exploration and travel

108 A visit to the Idrisi territory in 'Asir and Yemen.
Rosita Forbes. *Geographical Journal*, vol. 62 (1923), p. 271-8. map.

Part of this article is irrelevant, by nature of geography, but the account of the 'Asir province is useful.

109 Some recent Arabian explorations.
David George Hogarth. *Geographical Review*, vol. 11, pt. 3 (1921), p. 321-37.

An extremely useful survey article providing an overview of contemporary exploration.

110 War and discovery in Arabia.
David George Hogarth. *Geographical Journal*, vol. 55, pt. 4 (1920), p. 422-39.

This article illustrates how the involvement of the Middle East in the First World War led as a by-product to a greater geographical knowledge of the area.

111 A journey through central Arabia.
G. Leachman. *Geographical Journal*, vol. 43 (1914), p. 500-20. map (p. 604).

An account of a journey undertaken in 1912 from Damascus to Riyadh, in the hope of exploring the Rub' al Khali, which proved to be impassable. Nevertheless, a great deal of useful information was gathered from this restricted journey, and this is a valuable contemporary account.

112 A desert journey.
Trevor Mostyn. *Middle East International*, (Jan. 1978), p. 28-30.

An account of a journey through the 'Asir province into the empty quarter bordering on the Yemen. The author concludes that although a great deal of emphasis is being placed on industrialization, he wonders whether the planners 'would not do well to look to the Bedouin who are the last bearers of the true cultural identity of the peninsula'.

113 Across Arabia from the Persian Gulf to the Red Sea.
H. St. John B. Philby. *Geographical Journal*, vol. 56, pt. 4 (1920), p. 446-68. map.

An account of a journey from Uqair on the Gulf to Jeddah, made in 1919.

114 Arabian highlands.
H. St. John B. Philby. Ithaca, New York: Cornell University Press, 1952. 771p. maps.

An account of Philby's travels in the eastern province, mainly in the border areas between Saudi Arabia and the Yemen. This work contains a mass of topographical information about the 'Asir province, and detail as to the society and way of life in the area, as well as an account of the administration.

115 The empty quarter, being a description of the great south desert of Arabia known as Rub' al-Khali.

H. St. John B. Philby.   London: Constable, 1933. 433p. maps. Reprinted, Norwood, Pennsylvania: Norwood Editions.

This can be regarded as one of the classic accounts of exploration in the empty quarter, which is one of the really inhospitable areas of the world. It was traversed by Philby from north to south and from east to west.

116 The heart of Arabia: a record of travel and exploration.

H. St. John B. Philby.   London: Putnam, 1923. 2 vols. maps.

The record of St. John Philby's travels in the Nejd throughout 1917 and 1918; although many changes have taken place in the last fifty-five years, this can still be regarded as the best topographical guide to the area.

117 The land of Midian.

H. St. John B. Philby.   *Middle East Journal*, vol. 9, pt. 2 (1955), p. 117-29. map.

An account of a series of journeys made by St. John Philby into the northwestern Hedjaz, dealing mainly with the history of the area, its ancient sites and inscriptions, and the geography, especially with regard to the mapping of the area.

118 Rub' al Khali.

H. St. John B. Philby.   *Geographical Journal*, vol. 81, pt. 1 (1933), p. 1-26.

An account of a journey made in 1931 into the empty quarter, which is interesting both from the topographical and the anthropological aspects.

119 Sheba's daughters: being a record of travel in southern Arabia.

H. St. John B. Philby.   London: Methuen, 1939. 485p. map.

A further account of St. John Philby's explorations, as much of interest for its anthropological as for its topographical content.

120 Southern Najd.

H. St. John B. Philby.   *Geographical Journal*, vol. 55, pt. 3 (1920), p. 161-91. map.

An account of the author's journey from Riyadh in May 1919 to the south of Arabia, beginning with a description of Riyadh itself.

121 Through Wahhabiland on camelback.

Barclay Raunkiaer, edited by Gerald De Gaury.   London: Routledge & Kegan Paul; New York: Praeger, 1969. 156p. map.

An account of a journey made by the author from Kuwait in 1912, under the auspices of the Royal Danish Geographical Society. The journey was made in the eastern province of Saudi Arabia, and the author was received by the Imam Abdur-Rahman, father of Ibn Saud. The book gives a vivid picture of the Wahhabi movement and the discord in the area, and was rated by T. E. Lawrence as one of the best accounts of Arabian travel.

122 Arabian peak and desert: travels in al Yaman.

Amin F. Rihani. London: Constable, 1930. 280p.

Useful for a description of 'Asir province.

123 Around the coasts of Arabia.

Amin F. Rihani. London: Constable, 1930. 364p.

A good contemporary survey.

124 The Hejaz.

Eldon Rutter. *Geographical Journal*, vol. 77, pt. 2 (1931), p. 89-109. map.

A description of a visit made by the author in 1925, in the company of a pilgrim caravan, shortly after the Wahhabi occupation of the country. The author spent a year in the country, disguised as a pilgrim, and visited the holy places.

125 Tents and towers of Arabia.

Robert Shaffer. New York: Dodd, Mead, 1952. 276p. map.

A personal and sympathetic account of Saudi Arabia, based on the author's experiences, particularly in Jeddah.

126 Across the empty quarter.

Wilfred P. Thesiger. *Geographical Journal*, vol. 111, pt. 1-3 (1948), p. 1-21.

An account of the explorer's journey from Salalah in Oman across the Rub' al Khali to Liwa and back, a distance of some 2,000 miles. The journey was undertaken between October 1946 and May 1947 on behalf of the Middle East Anti-Locust Unit.

127 Arabian sands.

Wilfred P. Thesiger. London: Allen Lane, 1977. 347p. maps. (Originally published, London: Longman, 1959).

This must rank as one of the finest travel books about Arabia which, while being extremely readable, is full of detailed information about the topography, the flora and fauna, and the society of the areas explored. Some of the work is irrelevant, by nature of geography, dealing as it does with Oman and Abu Dhabi. Of great relevance are the accounts of Thesiger's two journeys across the empty quarter, and the picture that he paints of the tribes with whom he comes into contact, and the terrain through which he travelled. It is worth noting that the journeys were made by camel among Bedouin who had not been exposed to the effects of an oil-based economy, urbanization, or a society based on personal freedom and self-discipline.

128 A further journey across the empty quarter.

Wilfred P. Thesiger. *Geographical Journal*, vol. 113 (1949), p. 21-46.

An account of a journey through the western and northern areas of the Rub' al Khali between November 1947 and May 1948.

129 Across the Rub' al Khali.
Bertram Thomas. *Journal of the Royal Central Asian Society*, vol. 18, pt. 4 (1931), p. 489-504.

An account of Thomas's trip across the empty quarter.

130 Alarms and excursions in Arabia.
Bertram Thomas. London: Allen & Unwin, 1931. 296p.

A further account of the author's travels and exploits in the area of Saudi Arabia and Oman.

131 Arabia felix: across the empty quarter of Arabia.
Bertram Thomas. London: Cape, 1932. 304p.

This book ranks with the work of W. P. Thesiger as one of the classics on the exploration of Arabia. Although much of the work is concerned with the present-day sultanate of Oman, Thomas also explored in the 1930s the Rub' al Khali. The detailed description of his journey, his companions, and the tribesmen they met, present a valuable portrait of the area which is both sympathetic and objective.

132 A journey into Rub' al Khali - the southern Arabian desert.
Bertram Thomas. *Geographical Journal*, vol. 77, pt. 1 (1931), p. 1-38.

A further account of exploration of the empty quarter, with the author's usual precise detail and accurate observation.

133 The south-eastern borderlands of Rub' al Khali.
Bertram Thomas. *Geographical Journal*, vol. 73, pt. 3 (1929), p. 193-215.

The article studies the area within the present boundaries of Saudi Arabia, but also ventures into the sultanate of Oman. A classic account of exploration in this area.

134 A fool strikes oil: across Saudi Arabia.
Barbara Toy. London: Murray, 1957. 207p.

A readable travel account, which is interesting as it presents a feminine observation of a masculine society.

135 The highway of the three kings.
Barbara Toy. London: Murray, 1968. 188p. maps.

An account of a journey to trace the incense route from Bir Ali through Yemen and thence into Saudi Arabia. The route took the author to the outskirts of Mecca, and from there along the route of the Hedjaz railway to Petra, and then on to Damascus.

136 From Hasa to Oman by car.
D. F. Vesey-Fitzgerald. *Geographical Journal*, vol. 41, pt. 4 (1951), p. 544-60. map.

At the time of writing there was no published account of the entire route travelled by the author in 1947, and this is therefore of considerable interest. The author travelled extensively in the region as part of his duties with the Locust Control Centre.

137 **10,000 miles through Arabia.**
Ernst Wiese.   London: Hale, 1968. 191p. map.

An extremely readable account of a journey by car in Arabia, which also included a visit to Saudi Arabia, travelling from Dhahran to Taif. The author had an audience with King Faisal, and devotes a chapter to this meeting and his impressions of Riyadh.

Philby of Arabia.
See item no. 207.

Captain Shakespear: a portrait.
See item no. 250.

The holy cities of Arabia.
See item no. 299.

Jauf and the North Arabian desert.
See item no. 309.

The future of the north Arabian desert.
See item no. 694.

Geography

Physical geography

138 Some geographical aspects of al Riyadh.
M. T. Abul-Ela. *Bulletin de la Société de Géographie d'Egypte*, vol. 38 (1965), p. 31-72.

Studies the significance of the capital of Saudi Arabia in its geographical context. The first part deals with the physical environment, considering the geographical location and the Riyadh Basin complex, together with the geological confines of the settled area. Discussion of the water resources of the area includes details of the old water supply which came from wells sunk in the depression bed; some wells are still operative in the newer parts of Riyadh, operated by mechanical pumps. However, the main developments in Riyadh are now serviced by piped water from the pumping station at Ha'ir, using water drained from Wadi Hanifah. The author also considers the amounts of water provided, the storage facilities and analysis of the water itself. The latter section of the article deals with the development in detail of Riyadh as an urban centre. The urbanization is considered in three phases, 'firstly, the buildings that align the former paved roads and thoroughfares; secondly the residential suburbs which have sprung adjacent to some of the former locations; thirdly the infilling of the void spaces'. The article includes an account of the evolution of Riyadh up to the 19th century, and this is of historical interest because of Riyadh's importance as the capital.

139 Geographical observations in western Arabia.
Y. Abul-Haggag. *Bulletin de la Société de Géographie d'Egypte*, vol. 38 (1965), p. 81-96. maps.

An account of the geography of the west central plateau of Nejd and the 'Asir highlands, undertaken in the spring of 1962 and the winter of 1963, under the auspices of Riyadh University.

140 Arabian landscapes.
Aramco. *Viewpoints*, vol. 5, pt. 3 (1965), p. 3-10.

A general topographical article.

141 Sand formations in Southern Arabia.
R. A. Bagnold. *Geographical Journal*, vol. 117, pt. 1 (1951), p. 78-86. map.

A study of sand shapes, the length of their existence, and the present trend of development, seen in the light of a need for scientific study because of the requirement for roads, airstrips and oil installations.

142 The Middle East: a geographical study.
Peter Beaumont, G. H. Blake, J. M. Wagstaff. London, New York: Wiley, 1976. 572p. maps. bibliog.

This book opens with a discussion of the Middle East as a region, and this is followed by a study of the physical geography, geology and geomorphology. In this section Saudi Arabia is merely dealt with as part of the region, and is not included in the soil surveys which conclude the section. The sections on climate and water resources consider Saudi Arabia as part of the region as a whole; the former makes reference to weather systems, pressure and winds, temperatures, precipitation, and evapotranspiration, while the latter also includes specific discussion of Saudi Arabia, especially with regard to the importance of groundwater in the eastern province. The section dealing with petroleum in the Middle East considers the oil concessions, reserves, transportation, revenues, and future prospects. Each producing country also receives separate treatment, and so Saudi Arabia is dealt with in its own right, and also as part of the Saudi Arabia/Kuwait neutral zone. The closely linked sections dealing with problems of economic development and industry and trade are of particular importance. Among the problems considered are those of agriculture, population, and the lack of data necessary to plan economic development. As regards industry and trade, the author considers the resources available, the need for manufacturing industry, foreign trade, and internal trade and the problem of transportation. The section on rural land use is very significant because the role of agriculture is of fundamental importance. The organization of land use covers discussion of permanent settlements, the land tenure system, water rights, and pastoralism, while the patterns of land use cover discussion of nomadic grazing and cultivation. Population is dealt with briefly, due mainly to the lack of accurate statistical data from which to work. The demographic characteristics of the region are considered, as are migration and population distribution. The population is increasing rapidly, and is also undergoing radical structural change, especially in so far as the nomadic population is under considerable pressure to sedentarize. The problem of social change is covered in two sections, the first dealing with the 'traditional' socio-economic structure, and the second with modification and change, ending with a discussion of the influence of petroleum as an agent for change.

143 Eastern margin of the Red Sea and the coastal structures in Arabia.
G. F. Brown. *Philosophical Transactions of the Royal Society. A: Mathematical and Physical Sciences*, no. 1181, vol. 267 (1970), p. 75-88. maps.

A report of the results of the co-operative geological exploration programme of the U.S. Geological Survey and the Saudi Arabian government over a period of years commencing in 1950. The article considers the area by age, dealing with the paleozoic arch, mesozoic and early tertiary history, middle and late tertiary history and quaternary structure.

144 **Mineral occurrences related to stratigraphy and tectonics in tertiary sediments near Umm Lajj, eastern Red Sea area, Saudi Arabia.**
P. Dadet (and others). *Philosophical Transactions of the Royal Society. A: Mathematical and Physical Sciences*, no. 1181, vol. 267 (1970), p. 99-106. maps.

A report of the mineral occurrences near Umm Lejj in tertiary sedimentary strata, which, it is felt, are controlled by tectonic features following the direction of the Red Sea fault system. The hypothesis put forward is that the mineralization took place during the Red Sea depression.

145 **A discussion on the structure and evolution of the Red Sea, and the nature of the Red Sea, Gulf of Aden and Ethiopia Rift junction.**
Edited by N. L. Falcon (and others). *Philosophical Transactions of the Royal Society. A: Mathematical and Physical Sciences*, no. 1181, vol. 267 (1970), p. 99-106. maps.

146 **Reminiscences of the map of Arabia and the Persian Gulf.**
F. Fraser Hunter. *Geographical Journal*, vol. 53, pt. 4 (1919), p. 355-63.

The author was responsible for producing the maps to accompany John G. Lorimer's *Gazetteer of the Persian Gulf, Oman and Saudi Arabia* (q.v.).

147 **The structure of Asia.**
Edited by John Walter Gregory. London: Methuen, 1929. 227p.

A geological survey, including the Arabian peninsula.

148 **Arid lands: a geographical appraisal.**
Edited by E. Sherbon Hills. London: Methuen; New York: Barnes & Noble, 1966. 461p. maps.

This is a broadly based consideration of arid lands throughout the world, using illustrative material from various regions. Although based on much wider coverage than Saudi Arabia, this is still a useful work for that country.

149 **Desert geomorphology in the Arabian peninsula.**
Donald August Holm. *Science*, no. 3437, vol. 132 (1960), p. 1369-79. map.

The oil explorations in the Arabian peninsula have, as a by-product, produced geomorphic information which provides broad ideas as to the origin of the sand and rock areas of the peninsula but, in practice, more questions than answers to the various problems have emerged. Among problems considered are the emplacement of large sandy deserts, the tremendous variety of dune shapes, the origin of gravel plains, the age and geomorphic history of the Persian Gulf, the formation of sabkhahs and the tilting of the Arabian craton.

150 The geodetic survey of Saudi Arabia.
John Leatherdale. *Hunting Group Review*, vol. 72 (1970), p. 4-10. map.

A description of the establishment of a geodetic network as the first phase of the surveying and mapping programme for Saudi Arabia. The article discusses the technical and operational aspects of the work, and the nomadic existence of the survey teams.

151 Deserts of the world: an appraisal of research into their physical and biological environments.
Edited by W. G. McGinnies. Tucson, Arizona: University of Arizona Press, 1968. 788p. maps.

Although wider in coverage than the Middle East, this is still a useful work for studying the desert areas of Saudi Arabia.

152 Northern Nejd: a topographical itinerary.
A. Musil. New York: American Geographical Society, 1928. 367p. maps.

153 Saudi Arabia.
Focus (New York), vol. 16, pt. 9 (May 1966), 4p. map.

A survey of Saudi Arabia produced by the American Geographical Society, and aimed at providing introductory information on the country. Topics covered are physical geography, agriculture and settlement, oil, and industrial development and transportation.

154 A new map of Southern Arabia.
R. B. Sergeant, H. von Wissman. *Geographical Journal*, vol. 124, pt. 2 (1958), p. 163-71.

Mainly concerned with the Royal Geographical Society's new map covering Aden and present day Oman, and also the southern part of the Rub' al Khali. The first part of the article by von Wissman deals with cartography, while the contribution by Sergeant is concerned with the problems of transliteration and standardization of place-names.

155 The arid zones.
Kenneth Walton. London: Hutchinson; Chicago, Illinois: Aldine, 1969. 175p. maps.

An important contribution to the literature on the arid zones, including those of Saudi Arabia.

156 Mountains of Arabia.
L. Weiss. *Living Age*, no. 341 (1931), p. 149-54.

157 **Geology and geochemical reconnaissance of the Jabal al Haushak quadrangle, southern Nejd.**
J. W. Whitlow.   Jeddah: Ministry of Petroleum and Mineral Resources, 1968.

158 **Geology and geochemical reconnaissance of the Jabal al Shumrah quadrangle, southern Nejd.**
J. W. Whitlow.   Jeddah: Ministry of Petroleum and Mineral Resources, 1968.

Saudi Arabia.
See item no. 7.
Jiddah: portrait of an Arabian city.
See item no. 674.

Climatology

159 **Floods in Arabia and the western desert of Egypt.**
Meteorolgical Magazine, vol. 66 (1931), p. 64-5.
A note on abnormal weather conditions in the area of western Saudi Arabia, Transjordan and Egypt, explaining the reasons for the exceptional rainfall.

160 **A study of weather over the Arabian peninsula.**
W. S. Kuo.   *Meteorological Bulletin* (Taipei), vol. 11, pt. 2 (1965), p. 25-35.

161 **Saudi Arabia offers a rich potential of water development.**
Saudi Arabia. Ministry of Agriculture.   Washington, D.C.: Embassy of the Kingdom of Saudi Arabia, 1967.
Discusses water resources in Saudi Arabia and the potential for agricultural development.

162 **Arid zone meteorology.**
G. C. Wallen.   In: *Arid lands: a geographical appraisal.* Edited by E. S. Hills. London: Methuen; New York: Barnes & Noble, 1966, p. 31-52.

Saudi Arabia.
See item no. 7.

The Middle East: a geographical study.
See item no. 142.

Water resources and utilization

163 On the artesian water of Nejd, Saudi Arabia.
Y. Abul-Haggag. *Bulletin de la Société de Géographie d'Egypte*, vol. 39 (1966), p. 57-65.

In 1953 artesian water was found, by accident, in the north central part of Nejd at Buraida, the capital of Qassim Province. This discovery is considered to be an interesting feature in the physical and economic geography of Saudi Arabia. The article considers the geographical and maphological conditions in the area, and its geology and the programme of borings to exploit the water supply. The author concludes by considering the source of the water supply, which is hampered by a lack of geological and hydrological studies of the area, though it is felt that the main source area is to be found in the Hedjaz highlands in western Arabia. 'In the buried relief rather than in the subsurface structure, may lie the key to solving the problems of both the vertical and areal distribution of the artesian water of Qassim'.

164 New uses for ancient water.
Peter Beaumont. *Financial Times*, (10 June 1974).

A special report which discusses the irrigation and water utilization programme using underground freshwater sources.

165 Water and development in Saudi Arabia.
Peter Beaumont. *Geographical Journal*, vol. 143, pt. 1 (1977), p. 42-60. maps.

The author discusses the basis of the Saudi Arabian economy which, until recent years, was based on nomadic pastoralism and oasis agriculture, and the progress towards a rapid programme of development. This has brought problems, as industrialization has meant urbanization and a growing demand for water. The solution to this has been twofold, with exploitation of the deep aquifers in inland areas, and large desalination projects on the coast.

166 Ground water in the Nejd, Saudi Arabia.
R. A. Bramkamp, G. F. Brown. *Transactions of the New York Academy of Sciences*, vol. 2, pt. 10 (1948), p. 236-7.

A brief account of the potential of groundwater supplies, the exploitation of which is essential for any agricultural developments. It should be remembered, however, that the article is based on the information and the technology of thirty years ago.

167 **The geology and groundwater of Al Kharj district, Nejd, Saudi Arabia.**
G. F. Brown. *Transactions of the New York Academy of Sciences*, vol. 2, pt. 10 (1948), p. 370-5.

168 **Water in the desert.**
George B. Cressey. *Annals of the Association of American Geographers*, vol. 47, pt. 2 (June 1957), p. 105-24. map.
A general article about water in the desert areas, with various references to Saudi Arabia. The author considers the competition for water which exists in the desert, and hydrology in these regions. The problems of salt are also dealt with, as is the silting problem which can cause blocking or reduced efficiency in irrigation systems. The question of groundwater is dealt with, especially in relation to its exploitation, and this is linked to the future prospects for desert areas.

169 **The great Badanah flood.**
Daniel Da Cruz. *Aramco World*, vol. 18, pt. 4 (1967), p. 6-9.
Although the article does consider the problems of water in deserts generally, its main concern is the Wasia aquifer in eastern Saudi Arabia with its reserves of groundwater. Although the reserves are significant, the main problems to be faced are the construction of wells, supply systems for housing and irrigation, and the training of agriculturalists to exploit the irrigated farmland.

170 **Water supply, use and management.**
F. Dixey. In: *Arid lands: a geographical appraisal.* Edited by E. S. Hills. London: Methuen; New York: Barnes & Noble, 1966, p. 80-102.

171 **Water resources and land use in the Qatif oasis of Saudi Arabia.**
Charles H. V. Ebert. *Geographical Review*, vol. 55, pt. 4 (1965), p. 496-507. maps.
The eastern province of Saudi Arabia has a good supply of groundwater which crosses from the interior escarpment Zore to the wells of Al Qatif. At the time of the article only 25 per cent was utilized. The author examines the sources of groundwater and its utilization, and offers proposals for a more effective utilization of water and land.

172 **The oil-into-water miracle.**
Mohamed al-Feisal. *Geographical Magazine*, vol. 49, pt. 3 (Dec. 1976), p. 169-73. maps.
A discussion of the development programme of the Saline Water Conversion Corporation of Saudi Arabia. The first objective of the programme is to identify the natural resources, their potential, and the extent to which these will meet the future needs of the regions relying upon them. The programme also includes a consideration of future energy resources such as nuclear and solar energy. The short-term solutions are also discussed, in particular the current desalination programme in Saudi Arabia. The

company uses the flash desalination process; and on the Arabian Gulf coast natural gas is used as a fuel, whereas on the western coast heavy fuel is used. The author discusses the programme of the company and the phased production programme of plants.

173 Hydrological control of development in Saudi Arabia.

In: *Proceedings of the 23rd International Geological Congress Prague, 1968*, vol. 12, p. 145-53.

This paper illustrates the control exercised by the water supply on the economic and social development of the country.

174 Saudi Arabia - water supply of important towns.

Nazir Ahmad Jiabajee. *Pakistan Journal of Science*, vol. 9, pt. 5 (1957), p. 187-201. maps.

The article begins by considering the geology and climate of Saudi Arabia, since these factors determine the availability and suitability of water for drinking purposes. The towns considered are Jeddah, Medina, Mecca, Taif and Riyadh but, in addition, consideration is given to water supply arrangements on the Jeddah-Mecca road, from Yenbo to Medina, from Medina to Damascus, and on the Baghdad-Mecca road. Plans are produced of Saudi Arabia showing areas under consideration: Mecca, the aqueduct Aini Zubedha, and Medina. In each case the historical development of the water supply is traced, and the state of the supply at the time of the article is given.

175 Saudi Arabia plans for more fresh water.

I. Macdowell. *Arab World*, vol. 26 (1970), p. 14-15.

A short report on the desalination plant, north of Jeddah, designed to provide five million gallons of fresh water per day. In addition, a generating station adjacent to the plant will provide an additional 50,000 megawatts a day to the city. Brief mention is also made of a new desalination plant for al-Khabar on the Gulf coast, to supply water for that town and Dhahran and Dammam.

176 Some experiments with solar ground stills in Eastern Arabia.

J. Mandaville. *Geographical Journal*, vol. 138, pt. 1 (1972), p. 64-6.

An account of a trial to see whether solar stills could collect soil moisture for emergency desert water supplies. The experimenters at Dhahran were not successful, but it was found that the distillation of succulent plant matter could produce water. Also experiments on silty soil or salt marshes yielded an appreciable result, justifying the method for limited survival purposes.

177 Two notes from Central Arabia.

H. St. John B. Philby. *Geographical Journal*, vol. 113 (1949), p. 86-93.

An examination by Philby of the series of artesian lakes to be found in the Aflaj province of the Nejd, and the settlement evidence to be found in the area.

178 **Water resources and irrigation development in the Middle East.** C. G. Smith.
Geography, vol. 55, pt. 4 (1970), p. 407-25. maps.
A detailed consideration of the area as a whole, with supporting tables and maps to illustrate the water resources, land use, and irrigation programmes.

179 **A dam in Saudi Arabia.**
A. Yousif. *Aramco World*, vol. 25, pt. 2 (1974), p. 4-9.
A study of an important project in the Wadi Jaizan to construct a dam to harness the heavy seasonal rains which have hitherto been allowed to run off into the sands. The aim of the project is to ensure that agricultural land can be irrigated to allow the introduction of new crops and higher yields. In addition, the dam will eliminate the destructive flash floods which cause so much damage during the rainy seasons.

Some geographical aspects of al Riyadh.
See item no. 138.

The Middle East: a geographical study.
See item no. 142.

The nomad problem and the implementation of a nomadic settlement scheme in Saudi Arabia.
See item no. 426.

Saudi Arabia today.
See item no. 460.

Administrative reform in Saudi Arabia.
See item no. 482.

The economies of the Arab world: development since 1945.
See item no. 526.

Requiem for the empty quarter.
See item no. 576.

Saudi Arabia targets vast sums for development.
See item no. 656.

Maps

180 **Bartholomew world travel map: the Middle East.**
Edinburgh: Bartholomew, 1973. Scale 1:4,000,000.
This map and those listed in the following entries are all of value, though it should be noted that large areas of the kingdom have yet to be surveyed and the detail made available on published maps. A large number of the books listed in this bibliography contain maps of Saudi Arabia either as a separate country or as part of the Arabian peninsula. In particular mention should be made of *Kingdom of Saudi Arabia*, by Stacey International (q.v.), which contains several maps covering a variety of aspects relating to the kingdom. In addition some of the general guides such as the *Gulf handbook* (q.v.) town plans and these are also available from the relevant government ministries. One should also make mention of general atlases such as the *Times atlas of the world* and the *Oxford economic atlas*, which are not listed separately in this work.

Geography. Maps

181 **Arab world and Iran business map.**
London: Graham & Trotman, 1976. Scale 1:7,000,000.

Valuable for detail of oil fields, mineral deposits, ports, communications and major centres of population.

182 **Daily Telegraph map of the Middle East, India and Pakistan.**
London: Daily Telegraph [n.d.]. Scale 1:7,000,000.

Maps and atlases of the Middle East.
See item no. 779.

Flora and Fauna

183 **The deserts of Jafura and Jabrin.**
R. E. Cheesman. *Geographical Journal,* vol. 65, pt. 2 (1925), p. 112-41. map.

An expedition designed to study the fauna of the area, to bring back a collection of desert animals and birds, and to chart the distribution of resident birds, and the routes of migratory birds. The article is also useful for its topographical and descriptive content.

184 **A contribution to the flora of Saudi Arabia.**
Linnean Society Journal, no. 362, vol. 55 (1957), p. 632-43.

185 **Animals of the desert.**
E. B. Edney. In: *Arid lands: a geographical appraisal.* Edited by E. S. Hills. London: Methuen; New York: Barnes & Noble, 1966, p. 181-218.

186 **Plant life in deserts.**
M. Kassas. In: *Arid lands: a geographical appraisal.* Edited by E. S. Hills London: Methuen; New York: Barnes & Noble, 1966, p. 145-80.

187 **The vegetation of central and eastern Arabia.**
D. F. Vesey-Fitzgerald. *Journal of Ecology,* vol. 45, pt. 3 (1957), p. 779-98.

188 **Vegetation of the Red Sea coast north of Jeddah, Saudi Arabia.**
D. F. Vesey-Fitzgerald. *Journal of Ecology*, vol. 45, pt. 2 (1957), p. 547-62.

189 **Vegetation of the Red Sea coast, south of Jeddah, Saudi Arabia.**
D. F. Vesey-Fitzgerald. *Journal of Ecology*, vol. 43, pt. 2 (1955), p. 477-89.

190 **A contribution to the flora of Saudi Arabia.**
M. Zohary. *Linnean Society Journal*, no. 362, vol. 55 (1957), p. 632-43.
A listing of plants collected by the scientific staff of the Middle East Anti-Locust Research Unit between 1942 and 1945 in Saudi Arabia, and also in Oman. Included in the listing, which gives locations, are a number of species which were not previously recorded from Saudi Arabia.

191 **The flora of the desert to the south and west of Basra.**
M. Zohary. *Linnean Society Proceedings*, vol. 153 (1941), p. 98-108.

192 **On the Ghada tree of the northern Arabian and the Syrian desert.**
M. Zohary. *Palestine Journal of Botany*, vol. 1, pt. 4 (1940), p. 413-16.

Deserts of the world: an appraisal of research into their physical and biological environments.
See item no. 151.

Requiem for the empty quarter.
See item no. 576.

History

General

193 Lord of Arabia: Ibn Saud, an intimate study of a king.
Harold C. Armstrong. London: Penguin, 1938. 247p. maps.
bibliog. Reprinted, Mystic, Connecticut: Lawrence Verry.
A reprint of a title originally published in 1924. Little documentary evidence existed
for a biography of Ibn Saud and this book is based therefore on personal contact,
except for the writings of St. John Philby and Amin Rihani. In view of this and the
original publication date, the work is now dated, especially with regard to the
long-term influence of Ibn Saud. It is, however, very readable and a good introduction
to the early history of the house of Ibn Saud and Saudi Arabia.

194 Golden swords and pots and pans.
J. Arnold. London: Gollancz, 1964. 239p. map.
The autobiography of the former chief steward to King Saud.

195 Arabian destiny.
Jacques Benoist-Mechin. London: Elek, 1957. 298p. maps.
bibliog.
A life of Ibn Saud which traces the creation of the kingdom of Saudi Arabia from the
beginnings of the Wahhabi movement. The author considers Ibn Saud to be a man of
destiny and, although he is viewed in this light, the biography is extremely readable.

**196 Arabia, past and present. Volume 3: 'Asir before World
War I: a handbook.**
Sir Kinahan Cornwallis. Cambridge, England; New York:
Oleander Press, 1976. 155p. map.
Although somewhat dated, this is still useful for basic data and the historical back-
ground to the province. (Originally published in 1916 as *Handbook to 'Asir* by the
Arab Bureau).

197 Faisal: king of Saudi Arabia.

Gerald De Gaury. London: Arthur Barker, 1966. 191p. maps. bibliog.

A good biography of King Faisal written with his approval and co-operation and which, according to the author's note, aims 'to create understanding of the man, his background and his task'. The work is well illustrated, and the appendices reproduce extracts from King Faisal's speeches, and a plan of the Saudi Arabian administration. The author is a noted writer on Arabia in his own right, as well as a contributor to other people's works.

198 Rulers of Mecca.

Gerald De Gaury. London: Harrap, 1951. 317p.

Good introductory account of the house of Saud.

199 Vast areas neglected until now by archaeologists.

William Facey. *The Times* (London), (23 Sept. 1976), p. XI.

A *Times* special report which describes the moves to carry out archaeological studies in Saudi Arabia.

200 Britain and the Arabs: a study of fifty years, 1908-1958.

Sir John Bagot Glubb. London: Hodder & Stoughton, 1959. 496p. maps.

This work deals with the relations between Britain and the Arabs, and the early part with the First World War period, which includes a consideration of the rivalry between Hussein and Ibn Saud. The Nejd is dealt with separately (p. 207-15), giving a brief outline of the history and the rise of Wahhabism. This is followed by a study of Saudi Arabia following the discovery of oil (p. 351-60).

201 The desert king: a life of Ibn Saud.

David A. Howarth. London: Collins; New York: McGraw-Hill, 1964. 252p. bibliog.

A very good biography of Ibn Saud which is particularly valuable for its detailed consideration of the ruler's early life and, in particular, his links with the Wahhabi movement and the assumption of control over the Hedjaz, and the acceptance of guardianship of the holy places.

202 The isle of the Arabs.

Sheikh Inayatullah. *Islamic Culture*, vol. 2, pt. 2 (1937), p. 274-6.

The writer considers the location of Arabia, the various aspects of the location, and the effects of these aspects on the historical, commercial and racial development of the Arabs. The location of Arabia is of great significance to its development because it is an area of isolation, 'but in respect of its central position within a wide circle of lands, it becomes an intermediary between them as a focus, from which influences, if there be any, can radiate to great distances'.

203 **Britain and the Persian Gulf, 1795-1880.**
John B. Kelly. London, New York: Oxford University Press, 1968. 911p. maps. bibliog.

Although mainly concerned with Britain's activities in Kuwait, Bahrain and the so-called Trucial States, this is a relevant background book for the history of Saudi Arabia, particularly for the later border disputes.

204 **The harbinger of justice: biography of His Majesty King Abdul Aziz Ibn Saud.**
Abd al-Hamid al-Khalib. Karachi: al-Arab Printing Press, 1951. 2 vols.

This work, by a Saudi diplomat, was translated from the Arabic by E. Syed Irtizaali. As one would expect this is a sympathetic account, but it does contain historical data and information of great value.

205 **Arabia reborn.**
George I. Kheirallah. Albuquerque, New Mexico: University of New Mexico Press, 1952. 307p.

A general background of the history of the Arabian peninsula, and a personal impression of the changes that were taking place in Saudi Arabia in 1948.

206 **America and the Arabian peninsula: the first two hundred years.**
Joseph J. Malone. *Middle East Journal*, vol. 30, pt. 3 (1976), p. 406-24.

An account of relations between America and Saudi Arabia from the earliest contacts in the 18th century. Initial contact was by means of missionary stations and medical assistance, but the greatest impact came with the advent of oil and the growth of Aramco.

207 **Philby of Arabia.**
Elizabeth Monroe. London: Faber, 1973. 332p. maps. bibliog.

This biography of H. St. John B. Philby is an extremely important work and will be the standard work for many years to come. As Philby was one of the great explorers of Arabia and a close friend of Ibn Saud, this is also an account of the early history of Saudi Arabia and its exploration. The author also covers the early career of Philby; this spans the early days, with his involvement in Mesopotamia between 1915 and 1917, and his move thence into Arabia as political representative to Sir Percy Cox. This work has been exhaustively researched, with references to Philby's letters, survey notes, official documents, oil company records and the papers of the family, and as such is also a very valuable bibliographical record.

208 **Preliminary survey in N.W. Arabia, 1968.**
P. J. Parr, G. L. Harding, J. E. Dayton. *Bulletin of the Institute of Archaeology, University of London*, (1968-69), p. 193-243.

A report of an archaeological reconnaissance of north-west Saudi Arabia carried out in 1968, and the first official expedition from the United Kingdom. The area covered included the Midian and the northern Hedjaz, extending 250 kms. southwards from Aqaba and Muddawwerah to the latitude of al-Wajh on the Red Sea coast, to some 250 kms. inland. The survey is prefaced by a brief geographical sketch followed by the report of the survey dealing with the following locations: Khuraybah, Rawwafah and Qurayyah, with each report illustrated by line drawings and plates.

209 **Forty years in the wilderness.**
H. St. John B. Philby.   London: Hale, 1957. 272p. map.

An important work dealing with the history of Saudi Arabia as seen by a close confidant of the ruling family, especially Ibn Saud. It is the second volume of Philby's autobiography, following on from *Arabian days*. Although the book begins by describing his expulsion from Saudi Arabia, the bulk of the book is concerned with the early days of Ibn Saud's rule. In particular the book deals with the Arab revolt, especially the role of T. E. Lawrence and the invasion of the Hedjaz. Also as a thread through the book is the effect of oil on the Islamic strength of Saudi Arabia, which was even more vulnerable after the death of Ibn Saud. This event placed the country in danger not so much from within, but from political and nationalist influences from her neighbours.

210 **Saudi Arabia.**
H. St. John B. Philby.   London: Benn; Detroit, Michigan:
International Book Center, 1968. 358p.

An authoritative history of Saudi Arabia, containing a wealth of historical information, particularly on the life and traditions of the Bedouin. The book deals mainly with the changes effected by Ibn Saud, and in particular the conflicts that arose because of the opposition of a traditional religious society to changes that would enable the kingdom to relate to a secular modern world.

211 **The lost ruins of Quraiya.**
H. St. John B. Philby.   *Geographical Journal*, vol. 117, pt. 4
(1951), p. 448-58. map.

The ruins had been mentioned by previous explorers and one interpretation was that they were Ptolemy's Ostama. Philby has reservations about this but feels that it is probable that the site was a prosperous centre in Nabatean times.

212 **Ibn Saud of Arabia: his people and his land.**
Amin F. Rihani.   New York: Houghton Mifflin; London:
Constable, 1928, 370p.

A biography of Ibn Saud and an account of his kingdom, which had been expanded to include the Hedjaz. The book was published in America under the title *Maker of modern Arabia.*

213 **Faisal: the king and his kingdom.**
Vincent Sheean.   Tavistock, England: University Press of
Arabia, 1975. 161p.

The author has presented a detailed study of King Faisal and Saudi Arabia based not only on research but on his personal friendship with the King. The book traces the rise of the Saud family from the beginnings in the 18th century, with the rise of the Wahhabi movement and the struggle for dominance that followed. The creation of the kingdom of Saudi Arabia is then traced from the Saudi control of the Nejd to the taking of the Hedjaz and the arrival of the present-day kingdom. The oil question is also dealt with at length, particularly the relationship between the King and Aramco, the participation agreements, and the effects of the oil revenues on the economic and social life of the country. Above all, however, it is a portrait of a ruler who succeeded in creating the modern Saudi Arabia, and in ensuring stability despite pressures from within and without.

214 The emergence of the Middle East.
C. G. Smith. *Journal of Contemporary History*, vol. 3, pt. 3 (1968), p. 3-17.

This article is of interest for its picture of the historical development of the area from the beginning of the period of European involvement.

215 The birth of Saudi Arabia: Britain and the rise of the house of Sa'ud.
Gary G. Troeller. London: Cass, 1976. 287p. map. bibliog. (Distributed in the U.S.A. by International Scholarly Book Services, Forest Grove, Oregon).

This is a significant work which deals in detail with the early history of Saudi Arabia and, in particular, the role played by Britain in the rise to power of Ibn Saud. The work deals in detail with the Wahhabi movement, the alliance between the Wahhabis and the Saud family, and the gradual increase in Saudi control of the Nejd with the seizure of Hasa. Detailed consideration is also given to Anglo-Saudi relations during the war, with the treaty of non-alignment in return for a British subsidy, and with the rivalry between Ibn Saud and Hussein, together with a study of their relative importance in the Arab world. This is followed by a discussion of the dispute over Khurma and Turaba, and the role of the Ikhwan in these conflicts. Following the war British subsidies continued and Ibn Saud extended his control by ending the rule of the Rashids at Hail. However, conflict existed between Ibn Saud and his neighbours over the question of borders which involved Britain, due to her interests in Jordan, Iraq and the Gulf. The last chapter deals with the final conflict between Ibn Saud and Hussein, resulting in the capture of the Hedjaz by the Ikhwan. The appendices include a genealogy of the Saud family, the text of the Turko-Saudi treaty of 1914, and the drafts and final versions of the Anglo-Saudi treaty of 1915.

216 The wells of Ibn Saud.
D. Van Der Meulen. London: Murray, 1957. 270p.

The wells referred to in the title have three meanings; they refer firstly to oil, secondly to water, and thirdly to the spiritual wells of Wahhabism. The book traces the life of Ibn Saud and the history of Saudi Arabia while also portraying other key figures in the area, such as King Abdullah of Transjordan, St. John Philby, and Lawrence of Arabia. The author also deals with the impact of the American influence on the area, considering the changes and the consequences. In conclusion Van Der Meulen feels that the changes have mainly been for the worse. 'And what of its faith that now lies discarded by so many, sold for a mess of pottage? What is the spiritual future of the country to be?'.

217 Arabian days.
Sheikh Hafiz Wahba. London: Barker, 1964. 184p.

Through a series of essays the author portrays the historical, social and political development of Saudi Arabia, beginning with the people and their occupations, and the manners and customs of the region. Also dealt with is the development of medicine in Saudi Arabia, with reference to the conflict between modern medicine and the more traditional remedies. In considering the growth of education in the peninsula the author deals with the beginnings of schooling, and the effects of the ulema on the style and content of the educational programme. A large section of the work is concerned with the religious aspects of Saudi Arabia, in particular the religious revival in the Nejd and the rise of the Wahhabi movement. A significant contribution is the essay dealing with the Ikhwan and its influence throughout Arabia, not only in the religious but in the political field. The author also deals briefly with the history of the Saud family, the conquest of the Hedjaz, the rule of Ibn Saud, the moves towards modernization, and the attitudes of the traditional elements towards these changes.

218 **Survey starts on ancient riches.**
W. A. Ward, Mahmud Ghul. *The Times* (London), (28 Sept. 1970), p. IX.

Illustrated article on the beginning of archaeological surveys within Saudi Arabia to record and preserve her history.

219 **Ibn Saud: the puritan king of Arabia.**
Kenneth Williams. London: Cape, 1933. 299p.

This biography of Ibn Saud, aimed at the general reader, concentrates largely on the struggle to unite the present-day area of Saudi Arabia and to improve conditions among the Bedouin. These developments are described in relationship to the personal authority of the king as an individual, and the part played by the Wahhabi influences.

220 **Ancient records from North Arabia.**
F. V. Winnett, W. L. Reed. Toronto, London: University of Toronto Press, 1970. 264p.

The Middle East: a handbook.
See item no. 24.

Jiddah: portrait of an Arabian city.
See item no. 674.

Early history and the rise of Wahhabism

221 **The Arab's place in the sun.**
Richard Coke. London: Butterworth, 1929. 318p. maps.

This book deals with the role of the Arabs in the Middle East and world affairs. The second part deals with the national re-awakening, based on the Wahhabi movement with its spiritual re-awakening and a re-awakening of national identity. In the chapter on the First World War in the Middle East the author deals with the Arab revolt and, in particular, the political developments which were to determine the future of the area after the war. These developments, which were partially embodied in the Sykes-Picot treaty, are discussed in relation to the promises made to the Arabs, and particularly the differing policies of the Arab Bureau who supported Sherif Hussein, and the India Office who supported Ibn Saud.

222 The anatomy of the Saudi revolution.
David G. Edens. *International Journal of Middle East Studies*, vol. 5, pt. 1 (1974), p. 50-64.

In dealing with the changes that have taken place in Saudi Arabia the first part of the article examines the rise of Wahhabism and the collaboration between that movement and the house of Saud. 'The collaboration of these men and their descendants served to kindle a flame in the minds of the Bedouin and to spread Saudi dominion'. The author continues by describing the rise to power of Ibn Saud, the conflict between the house of Saud and the Rashid family, and the gradual welding of the tribes into a cohesive nation, ending in the declaration of the kingdom of Saudi Arabia in 1932. The period following was one of internal consolidation, though it was not without problems, due to difficulties with the Ikhwan. Together with these power developments, however, there were significant economic and social developments. These did not, however, come as a result of income from oil, which really began to have an impact after the Second World War.

223 The Arab revival.
Franceso Gabrielli. London: Thames & Hudson, 1961. 178p. maps.

Relevant for a consideration of the Wahhabi movement in the 19th century.

224 Arab nationalism: an anthology.
Edited by Sylvia G. Haim. Los Angeles, London: University of California Press, 1962. New ed., 1976. 255p. bibliog.

A valuable work which is essential to any study of Arab nationalism, though the only relevant section here is that dealing with Wahhabism and Islam as factors in the rise of Arab nationalism.

225 The later Ottoman empire in Egypt and the fertile crescent.
P. M. Holt. In: *Cambridge history of Islam. Vol. 1: The central Islamic lands*. London, New York: Cambridge University Press, 1970, p. 374-93.

This article deals with the rise of the Wahhabi movement and the challenge that it presented to the structure of the Ottoman empire, both in the spiritual and political senses. The movement was defeated during a series of campaigns between 1811 and 1818 which forced the Wahhabis out of the Hedjaz and broke the power of the house of Saud in the Nejd.

226 Arabic thought in the liberal age, 1789-1939.
Albert H. Hourani. London: Oxford University Press for the Royal Institute of International Affairs, 1962. New ed., 1970. 403p. bibliog.

The definitive account of Arab intellectual history which is important here for its examination of the Wahhabi movement.

History. Early history and the rise of Wahhabism

227 The Arab world: past, present and future.
Nejla Izzeddin. Chicago: Henry Regnery, 1953. 412p.

The latter part of this work deals with the rise of the Wahhabi movement in the Nejd and the religious concept of the movement, together with the links with the Saud family.

228 A diplomat's report on Wahhabism of Arabia.
Mu'Iruddin A. Khan. *Islamic Studies*, vol. 7, pt. 1 (1968), p. 33-46.

The text of a report Sir Harford Jones Brydges, the British Resident at Baghdad, made in 1799 on the Wahhabi movement. This is of particular interest because it is one of the earliest accounts of the movement by a European.

229 The Middle East and the West.
Bernard Lewis. London: Weidenfeld & Nicolson, 1964. Reprinted, 1968. 164p. bibliog.

In the chapter entitled 'The revolt of Islam' the author deals with the significance of the Wahhabi movement. 'At a time when the Ottoman empire was suffering defeat and humiliation at the hands of Christian enemies, the Wahhabi revolution marks a first withdrawal of consent from Ottoman Turkish supremacy'.

230 Arab political movements.
Peter Mansfield. In: *The Middle East: a political and economic survey*. Edited by Peter Mansfield. 4th ed. London, New York: Oxford University Press, 1973, p. 66-90.

Discusses the awakening of the Arab national consciousness in the 19th century.

231 Religion and politics in Arabia.
Alois Musil. *Foreign Affairs* (New York), vol. 6, pt. 4 (1928), p. 675-81.

A discussion of the role of Wahhabism in the creation of the empire of Saudi Arabia, and the problem faced by Ibn Saud in reconciling the aspirations of the Ikhwan with the political realities of Arabia. Particular reference is made to the activities of the Ikhwan in raids into Jordan and Iraq; both of these were British mandated territories, and therefore strains were placed upon the treaty between Britain and Ibn Saud.

232 Arabia.
H. St. John B. Philby. London: Benn, 1930. 387p. map.

A general survey of the modern history of the Arabian peninsula, concentrating mainly on the rise and influence of the Wahhabi movement, and its relationship with the house of Saud.

233 A survey of Wahhabi Arabia.
H. St. John B. Philby. *Journal of the Royal Central Asian Society*, vol. 16 (1929), p. 468-72.

234 **Wahhabism and Saudi Arabia.**
George Rentz. In: *The Arabian peninsula: society and politics*. Edited by Derek Hopwood. London: Allen & Unwin; Lotowa, New Jersey: Rowman & Littlefield, 1972, p. 54-66.

This essay examines the Wahhabi movement which became synonymous with the state of Saudi Arabia and, although this name was not adopted until 1932, the author contends that the state was both Wahhabi and Saudi from 1744, though with brief interruptions. The author briefly considers Arabia at the beginning of the 18th century and the founding of the Wahhabi movement. This is followed by the alliance with the house of Saud, and the spread of Wahhabism, followed by the rise in power of the movement, leading to the intervention of Muhammad Ali and the fall of the Wahhabi state in 1818. The Wahhabi state went through two periods of revival, only to fall into obscurity again with the rise to power of the Rashid from 1891 to 1902. The essay concludes with a consideration of Wahhabism in the 20th century and its relations with the Islamic world.

235 **The social composition of the military in the process of state formation in the Arabian desert.**
Henry Rosenfeld. *Journal of the Royal Anthropological Institute*, vol. 95, pt. 1 (1965), p. 75-86.

This article deals specifically with the dynasty of the Ibn Rashid at Hail during the period from 1830 to 1900. The social composition of the military is seen as a key to the understanding of the lack of development of a society as 'the process of state formation is dependent on the development of an exclusive instrument of force, a military...'. The article is divided into two sections, the first dealing with the social environment and the interaction of warrior nomads and settlers, and the second with the economic basis for the development of the state of Ibn Rashid at Hail.

236 **The Arab federalists of the Ottoman empire.**
Hassan Saab. Amsterdam: Djambaton, 1958. 322p. bibliog.

The Wahhabi movement is considered to have been the most lasting of the early nationalistic movements within the Ottoman empire. Although the movement was defeated by Muhammad Ali it was not destroyed, and it became a unifying force welding together a multiplicity of tribes within the Nejd.

237 **Arab unity: hope and fulfilment.**
Fayez A. Sayegh. New York: Devin-Adair, 1958. 272p.

A study of the concept of Arab unity in the modern Arab world. This work also deals with the rise of the Arab nationalist movement, particularly with regard to Wahhabism.

238 **Arabs and Turks.**
J. F. Scheltema. *Journal of the American Oriental Society*, vol. 37 (1917), p. 153-61.

The article considers the rise of the puritan Islamic movement of the Wahhabi, its initial defeat by Muhammad Ali, and its subsequent influence in Arabia.

239 The Wahhabis in western Arabia in 1803-04 A.D.
R. B. Sergeant, G. M. Wickens. *Islamic Culture*, vol. 23 (1949), p. 308-11.

An account of the rise of the Wahhabi movement and its impact on the politics of the area, and as a reforming force within Islam.

240 The Wahhabis and Ibn Saud.
W. F. Smalley. *Moslem World*, vol. 22, pt. 3 (1932), p. 227-46.

An account of the historical development of Wahhabism as a political force, and the religious doctrine of the movement. The rise of the movement is also dealt with in relation to the fortunes of the Saud family, and the struggle for control of the Nejd.

241 The rise of the Wahhabi power and the delimination of frontiers.
Sir Arnold Toynbee. In: *Survey of international affairs. Vol. 1*. Edited by Sir Arnold Toynbee. London: Oxford University Press for the Royal Institute of International Affairs, 1925. 611p.

Indispensable for a study of Anglo-Saudi relations.

242 Wahhabism in Arabia, past and present.
Sheikh Hafiz Wahba. *Journal of the Royal Central Asian Society*, vol. 16, pt. 4 (1929), p. 458-67.

The text of a lecture, by a close associate of Ibn Saud, to a British audience, on the historical development and doctrinal content of Wahhabism.

243 Arabia and Islam.
Kenneth Williams. *Contemporary Review*, (Jan. 1926), p. 55-60.

This article is concerned with the impact of Islam, in the form of Wahhabism, on Arabia under the guidance of Ibn Saud and, in particular, its impact upon Islam in Saudi Arabia. Also considered is the invasion of the Hedjaz by the Ikhwan, and the expulsion of the Sherifians from the holy places.

244 Saudi Arabia in the nineteenth century.
Richard Bayly Winder. London: Macmillan, 1965. 312p. maps. bibliog.

A popular history of the areas that now form Saudi Arabia and, in particular, the Saudi family and its position as the ruling family.

245 Arab-Turkish relations and the emergence of Arab nationalism.

Zeine N. Zeine. Beirut: Khayat's, 1966. 2nd ed. 156p. bibliog.

The Wahhabi movement is considered as part of the rise of anti-Turkish sentiment in Arab lands, largely beginning as a desire for independent local government within the Ottoman empire, before becoming a movement which represented a threat to the Sublime Porte.

246 The Wahhabis: their origins, history, tenets and influences.

S. M. Zwemer. *Journal of the Transactions of the Victoria Institute*, vol. 33 (1901), p. 311-30.

Although dated, useful for contemporary background.

The Near East: a modern history.
See item no. 73.

Some geographical aspects of al Riyadh.
See item no. 138.

Lord of Arabia: Ibn Saud, an intimate study of a king.
See item no. 193.

The birth of Saudi Arabia: Britain and the rise of the house of Sa'ud.
See item no. 215.

Captain Shakespear: a portrait.
See item no. 250.

Britain's moment in the Middle East, 1914-56.
See item no. 293.

The House of Saud to World War I

247 The Arab War.

Gertrude Lothian Bell. London: Golden Cockerel Press, 1940. 52p.

A series of articles written between October 1916 and July 1917 for the Arab Bureau in Cairo, which first appeared as secret despatches in the *Arab Bulletin*. Its significance lies in the background information that it provides with regard to the situation in the Middle East at the time of the outbreak of the Arab Revolt. Of relevance here are the studies of Turkish rule in Arabia, the importance of Ibn Saud, and the position of the Rashids of Hail.

248 The affairs of Arabia, 1905-1906.

Great Britain. Foreign Office Confidential Print, edited by Robin L. Bidwell. London: Cass, 1971. 8 vols. in 2.

Although mainly concerned with Kuwait the volumes also cover other aspects of the Arabian peninsula including the struggle of Ibn Saud for supremacy in the Nejd.

249 Lawrence of Arabia: the work behind the legend.

H. St. John B. Philby. *Review of Reviews*, (June 1935), p. 15-17. map.

The main thread of the article is a discussion of the basic error of British policy regarding the revolt of the Arabs against the Turks, that of supporting the Sherifian family instead of Ibn Saud.

250 Captain Shakespear: a portrait.

H. V. F. Winstone. London: Cape, 1976. 236p. maps. bibliog.

As political agent in Kuwait, Shakespear actively supported the cause of Ibn Saud as the natural leader of the tribes against the Turks. However, pressure from the India Office was not successful as British support was given to Hussein and Ibn Saud was left to maintain sympathetic neutrality supported by a British subsidy. However, during the war Shakespear was sent to Arabia to ensure that the tribes did not enter the war on the Turkish side. He was killed whilst accompanying Ibn Saud in battle against Ibn Rashid of Hail. His exploits as an explorer are relatively unknown, as they have been eclipsed by the achievements of Philby, Burton, Doughty, etc., but this book documents his travels in the Nejd at the beginning of the 20th century.

The Near East: a modern history.
See item no. 73.

Britain and the Arabs: a study of fifty years, 1908-1958.
See item no. 200.

The birth of Saudi Arabia: Britain and the rise of the house of Sa'ud.
See item no. 215.

Arabian days.
See item no. 217.

Saudi Arabia (Islam in politics).
See item no. 393.

A house built on sand: a political economy of Saudi Arabia.
See item no. 447.

Riyadh and the central province.
See item no. 518.

Anglo-Saudi relations during World War I

251 The letters of Gertrude Lothian Bell. Vol. 2.

Gertrude Lothian Bell. London: Benn, 1927. 387p. map.

The second volume is important for contemporary insights into Anglo-Saudi relations.

252 Shifting sands.

N. N. E. Bray. London: Unicorn Press, 1934. 312p. maps.
Reprinted, New York: AMS Press.

Although mainly concerned with the Arab revolt, the author also deals with British support for Hussein instead of Ibn Saud, and the whole question of the future of Arabia on the basis of conflicting promises and agreements.

253 Britain, India and the Arab, 1914-1921.

Briton Cooper Busch. Berkeley, California; London:
University of California Press, 1971. 522p. maps. bibliog.

A detailed account of the complex problems facing Britain in the Middle East during and after the war, particularly the Arab revolt, and promises to the Arabs in relation to the Sykes-Picot agreement. The author introduces the complicated element of the British government in India, which was concerned with influence in the Persian Gulf, and this meant support for Ibn Saud's position in the Nejd. The role of India in Britain's relations with the Arab world during this crucial period is seen as contributing detrimentally to future relations with the independent Arab states.

254 Arabia and the Arabs.

Sir Gilbert Clayton. *Journal of the Royal Institute of International Affairs,* (Jan. 1929), p. 8-20.

The major part of this article deals with Britain's position in Arabia prior to the First World War, the political conduct of the war, the political aspects of the peace settlement, and the operation of the mandates. Consideration is given to relations between Ibn Saud and Britain (with whom he had maintained friendly relations) which were soured by the support already given to Hussein. The author maintains, however, that Britain did not make an incorrect choice in backing Hussein as 'the two horses ran at the same meeting, they did not run in the same race.... Ibn Saud could not have influenced the course of operations in Palestine any more than Hussein could have helped us in Mesopotamia'. The article also deals with postwar relations between the Hashemites and Ibn Saud, which resulted in the invasion of the Hedjaz by the Ikhwan, and the eventual incorporation of the territory into the Nejd. As a result of these changes Ibn Saud assumed control of the stage.

255 Correspondence between Sir Henry McMahon, His Majesty's Commissioner at Cairo, and the Sherif Hussein of Mecca, July 1915-March 1916, with map.

Great Britain. Foreign Office. London: H.M. Stationery Office, 1939. 18p. map. (Cmd. 5957).

This publication does not specifically relate to Saudi Arabia, but it is of vital importance to any understanding of Anglo-Saudi relations and of the subsequent rivalry between Ibn Saud and Hussein. A study of each of the ten letters is essential for an understanding of these aspects of Saudi Arabian history.

256 **Diplomacy in the Near and Middle East: a documentary record, 1535-1956. Vol. II: 1914-1956.**
Jacob C. Hurewitz. London: Van Nostrand, 1956. 427p.
Reprinted, New York: Octagon Books.

A collection of documents relating to diplomacy in the area during the period in question; of particular relevance is the British treaty with Ibn Saud of 26 December 1915, which appears on page 17.

257 **England and the Middle East: the destruction of the Ottoman empire, 1914-1921.**
Elie Kedourie. London: Bowes & Bowes, 1956. 236p.
bibliog.

An important work for the consideration of British policy in the Middle East prior to and during the First World War. It examines in detail the support for the Sherifian cause, and the other political agreements concluded between the Allies while the Arab revolt was in progress.

258 **Downing Street and the Arab potentates.**
'L'. *Foreign Affairs*, vol. 6 (1927), p. 233-40.

A consideration of the relationships between Britain and the Arab states based on treaties of friendship and financial subsidies. The article considers in detail the reasons for granting financial aid to both Hussein and Ibn Saud.

259 **The letters of T. E. Lawrence.**
Thomas Edward Lawrence, edited by David Garnett. London: Cape, 1938. 896p.

The early sections are of interest here, particularly the letters dealing with the reasons for supporting the Hashemites, the conduct of the war, and the peace conference and the future of Arabia.

260 **Evolution of a revolt: early postwar writings of T. E. Lawrence.**
Thomas Edward Lawrence, edited by Stanley Weintraub, Rodelle Weintraub. University Park, Pennsylvania; London: Pennsylvania State University Press, 1968. 175p. maps.

This work contains Lawrence's miscellaneous pieces, which appeared as a series of newspaper and periodical articles between 1918 and 1921. It is mainly of interest here for the background to the events between the outbreak of the Arab revolt and the peace conference.

261 **Revolt in the desert.**
Thomas Edward Lawrence. London: Cape, 1927. 446p. maps.

An abridgement of *The seven pillars of wisdom*, and basically a straightforward account of the revolt, without the introspection of the larger work.

262 **The seven pillars of wisdom: a triumph.**

Thomas Edward Lawrence. London: Cape; New York:
Doubleday, 1935. 702p. maps.

The full account of the Arab revolt with Lawrence's own personal insights. Useful
mainly for the political background.

263 **Arabia of the Wahhabis.**

H. St. John B. Philby. London: Constable, 1928. 422p. map.

A further account of Philby's stay in Saudi Arabia, concentrating on the period
1917-18 and therefore greatly concerned with the position of Ibn Saud in the First
World War, the Arab revolt and relations with the Hashemites. In addition there are
the detailed accounts of Philby's travels during this period.

264 **Arabia today.**

H. St. John B. Philby. *International Affairs*, vol. 14, pt. 5
(1935), p. 619-34.

The first part of this article deals with the position of Saudi Arabia during the First
World War and, in particular, with the moves by the Allies to secure Arab support for
the war against the Turks. The author moves on to discuss the period after the end of
the war, and the various conferences to determine the fate of the Middle East, a time
which saw increasing friction between Ibn Saud and his Hashemite neighbours. Philby
was in Transjordan at the time of the conference held in April 1924 to settle the
problems of the area, and he forecast the invasion of the Hedjaz by Ibn Saud if
agreement was not reached. 'But the British government were almost less inclined to
listen to me than they had been...and they stuck to their guns. In September 1924 Ibn
Saud started his campaign...and within a year was King of the Hedjaz.' The final part
of the article deals with the consolidation of the kingdom of Saudi Arabia by Ibn Saud
and, in particular, with relations between Great Britain and Saudi Arabia; these were
coloured by the need for an air route to India and by the presence of oil. The latter
factor was complicated by ill-defined boundaries between Saudi Arabia and the Gulf
states, where Britain had interests and influence.

265 **Report on the Nejd mission October 29 1917-November 1 1918.**

H. St. John B. Philby. Baghdad: Government Press, 1918.
53p.

An account of the negotiations leading to a treaty between Great Britain and Ibn Saud,
together with the text of the treaty.

266 **The emergence of the Middle East, 1914-1924.**

Howard M. Sachar. London: Allen Lane; New York: Knopf,
1969. 518p. maps. bibliog.

The crucial years from the outbreak of the First World War to the mandatory period
following the San Remo Conference. The one section of direct relevance to Saudi
Arabia is that dealing with the Arab revolt and the negotiations with the Allies, which
are related to the rivalry between Hussein and Ibn Saud.

267 Ibn Saud and Sherif Hussein: a comparison in importance in the early years of the First World War.

Gary G. Troeller.   *Historical Journal*, vol. 14, pt. 3 (1971), p. 627-33.

A significant article which examines the whole question of the relative importance of Hussein and Ibn Saud during the First World War. The author concludes that the whole question can only be discussed in the light of conditions current at that time, and not in retrospect. The author rejects the view of Philby that Ibn Saud was the logical choice because of Hussein's influence as a religious leader, Abdullah's contact with Ottoman Arab officers through the secret societies, and the role of the Hedjaz in providing added protection to Egypt and the troop corridor from India. On the other hand Ibn Saud headed the Wahhabi movement which was feared by many Muslims, and at that time he did not command the same authority as the Sherif of Mecca. Politically Ibn Saud's influence did not extend beyond central and eastern Arabia and, although he neutralized Ibn Rashid's support for the Turks, Hussein could potentially occupy the attention of four Turkish divisions in the Hedjaz. It is, the author concludes, only the subsequent career of Ibn Saud which could lead one to believe that politically Britain made the wrong choice.

268 Gertrude Bell.

H. Victor F. Winstone.   London: Cape, 1978. 344p.

The first woman to make the expedition to Hail on her own (in 1913). Gertrude Bell was a member of the Arab Bureau. Her influence was considerable, notably in the part she played in obtaining the election of Faisal ibn Hussein as king of Iraq, and her support of the Hashemites.

269 The Arab lands, 1918-1948.

Zeine N. Zeine.   In: *Cambridge history of Islam. Vol. 1: The central Islamic lands*. London, New York: Cambridge University Press, 1970, p. 566-94.

Not all of this article is relevant as it deals extensively with Palestine and the mandated territories. It does, however, deal with the period leading up to the Arab revolt, and also the clashes between Hussein and Ibn Saud.

Lord of Arabia: Ibn Saud, an intimate study of a king.
See item no. 193.

The birth of Saudi Arabia: Britain and the rise of the house of Sa'ud.
See item no. 215.

The Arab's place in the sun.
See item no. 221.

From Ottomanism to Arabism: essays on the origins of Arab nationalism.
See item no. 278.

The Chatham House version and other Middle-Eastern studies.
See item no. 286.

In the Anglo-Arab labyrinth: the McMahon-Husayn correspondence and its interpretations, 1914-1939.
See item no. 287.

Saudi-Hashemite rivalry

270 **Memoirs of King Abdullah of Transjordan.**
Abdullah I, edited by Philip R. Groves.   London: Cape, 1950.
278p.
Relevant to the study of relations between the Saudi and Sherifian families, especially
in relation to the border problems between Saudi Arabia and Transjordan. The problem
was caused mainly by Ibn Saud's fear of being surrounded by Hashemite-controlled
territory, and by Abdullah's reactions to the situation in the Hedjaz.

271 **The Arab awakening: the study of the Arab nationalist
movement.**
George Antonius.   London: Hamish Hamilton; New York:
Putnam, 1938. 471p. maps.
During the war Hussein had been supported by Britain while Ibn Saud's neutrality had
been guaranteed by means of subsidies. After the peace settlement British support for
Hussein was withdrawn, due to his intransigence over treaty negotiations with the
British government. Also Hussein was unable to handle relationships with Ibn Saud, as
he felt that the leadership of the Arab revolt and the position of Sherif of Mecca gave
him political ascendancy over the Arab nations. As a result Hussein treated the border
disputes with Ibn Saud in a high-handed and provocative manner, and the result was
the Wahhabi invasion of the Hedjaz in 1924. The expected British support did not
materialize, and Hussein was forced to abdicate in favour of Ali; but defeat was
inevitable, and by December 1925 Ibn Saud controlled the Hedjaz and the holy places.

272 **Middle East: past and present.**
Yahya Armajani.   Englewood Cliffs, New Jersey; London:
Prentice-Hall, 1970. 432p. maps. bibliog.
Section IV, entitled 'The modern Middle East', deals in part with the fertile crescent
under mandate, and in this section the rivalry between Hussein and Ibn Saud is
examined, including the capture of the Hedjaz. The last chapter examines Arab unity
and disunity in the 20th century, and Saudi Arabia is covered in a general survey of
inter-state relations in the Arab world.

273 **The early Wahhabis and the Sherifs of Makkah.**
Muhammad Abdul Bari.   *Journal of the Pakistan Historical
Society*, vol. 3 (1953), p. 91-104.
An examination of the long series of rivalries and wars between the Wahhabis and the
Sherifs of Mecca, which ended in the occupation of the Hedjaz by the forces of Ibn
Saud. The article examines the position and role of the Sherifian family as protectors

of the holy places, the rise of the Wahhabi movement, and the resultant conflict between the two factions.

274 **The Middle East: crossroads of history.**
E. Ben-Horin.   New York: W. W. Norton, 1943. 248p. map.
Mainly concerned with the problems of Arab unity and in particular the question of Pan-Arabism versus Pan-Islamism.

275 **Documents on British foreign policy, 1919-1939. First Series. Vol. XIII. The Near and Middle East, January 1920-March 1921.**
Edited by Rohan Butler, J. P. T. Bury.   London: H.M. Stationery Office, 1963. 747p.
Provides general background to this period, and specifically (p. 215ff.) documents relating to the rivalry between Hussein and Ibn Saud.

276 **Arabia and the Arabs.**
Sir Gilbert Clayton.   *Journal of the Royal Instute of International Affairs*, (Jan. 1929), p. 8-20.
The article briefly covers the background to the Hussein-Ibn Saud rivalry prior to 1916. Relations deteriorated after Ibn Saud's victory over the Rashids in 1921, owing to Hussein's arrogance, 'and the reactionary nature of his rule had alienated many of his people and undoubtedly weakened his own position' thus ensuring his defeat after the Wahhabi invasion of the Hedjaz.

277 **An Arabian diary.**
Sir Gilbert Clayton, edited by Robert O. Collins.   Los Angeles, London: University of California Press, 1969. 379p. bibliog.
The introductory section considers the roots of dissent between Hussein and Ibn Saud, which were accentuated by the support given to Hussein through the Arab Bureau and to Ibn Saud through the India Office. The remainder of the section deals with the stalemate during the First World War, the border disputes following the war, and the invasion of the Hedjaz by Ibn Saud.

278 **From Ottomanism to Arabism: essays on the origins of Arab nationalism.**
C. Ernest Dawn.   Urbana, Illinois; London: University of Illinois Press, 1973. 212p.
Although concerned with the Arab revolt and the role of Hussein in the evaluation of Arab nationalism, the earlier essays are also of relevance to the rivalry between the Hashemites and Ibn Saud.

279 The crescent in crisis: an interpretive study of the modern Arab world.
Nabih Amin Faris, Mohammed Husayne. Lawrence, Kansas: University of Kansas Press, 1955. 191p.

In dealing with the factors which legislate against national unity in the Arab world, the question of dynastic rivalries is discussed, particularly in relation to the rivalries between Ibn Saud and the Hashemites, both with each other and in their dealings with the great powers.

280 Lawrence and King Hussein: the 1921 negotiations.
Z. Gaster. *National Review* (15 Oct. 1918), p. 512-5.

This article discusses the attempts made by T. E. Lawrence to negotiate a treaty with Hussein, but the treaty was not signed as the proposals ignored Hussein's aspirations to a wider Arab empire.

281 Arab unity: ideal and reality.
Harold W. Glidden. In: *The world of Islam.* Edited by James Kritzeck and R. Bayley.

The quest for Arab unity after the war is seen in the light of the rivalry between Hussein and Ibn Saud, which was also accentuated by the Hashemite control over the holy places. This rivalry also defeated moves to found an Arab caliphate and resulted in the invasion of the Hedjaz. The author feels that Arab unity was never a reality, the real obstacle being internal Arab tensions rather than foreign intrigue.

282 The foundation of the League of Arab States.
Ahmed M. Gomaa. London: Longman, 1977. 323p. bibliog.

This work, in dealing with the background leading up to the foundation of the League of Arab States, considers the historical evaluation of Arab nationalism from the First World War, and deals in part with the rivalry between Hussein and Ibn Saud, and subsequent relations with Abdullah's rule in Transjordan and ambitions in Syria. The coverage of the Second World War includes explanation of the role played by Ibn Saud in relations between the Arabs and the Axis powers, and, especially, in relations with Britain. 'He wanted to foil the moves of the Hashemites, and to vindicate, by his favourable influence on the neighbouring Arabs, his worth as a good friend of the British.' Discussion of the Arab unity consultations covers the relations between Ibn Saud and Nuri al-Sa'id, and the mistrust with which Ibn Saud viewed the latter's scheme for Arab unity. As regards the possibility of an Arab federation, it was argued that there was nothing to show that Arab opinion was ready for such a move, nor would Ibn Saud be persuaded to assume its leadership because of Palestine. However, the various tentative moves eventually led to the founding of the League of Arab States in 1945, as a result of Arab initiative encouraged by Britain.

283 Report on the Middle East Conference, Cairo and Jerusalem, March 12th to 30th 1921, with appendix.
Great Britain. Colonial Office. London: H.M. Stationery Office, 1921. 210p.

The official account of the Cairo Conference giving the background to the conference, a report on the discussions, and its recommendations. Mainly of interest for areas other than Saudi Arabia, but of relevance here because the conference decided the boundaries and future of territories bordering on Saudi Arabia and, in particular, the future of the Hashemites.

284 **The partition of Turkey: a diplomatic history, 1913-1923.**
Harry N. Howard.   New York: Howard Fertig, 1966. 486p.
maps.

In dealing with the period following the peace settlement and the granting of the mandates, this work also considers the rivalry between Hussein and Ibn Saud in the light of the differing British foreign policies in the area.

285 **The revolt in Arabia.**
C. Snouck Hurgronje.   New York: Putnam, 1917. 50p.

Not strictly concerned with Saudi Arabia but included because of the account of the Sherifate of Mecca and its place in the structure of the Ottoman empire. An understanding of this is essential to an understanding of the attitude of Ibn Saud towards Sherifian administration of the holy places.

286 **The Chatham House version and other Middle-Eastern studies.**
Elie Kedourie.   London: Weidenfeld & Nicolson; New York:
Praeger, 1970. 488p. bibliog.

The chapter on p. 33-47 deals with the negotiations between Britain and the Arabs over Arab participation in the war against the Turks. Although primarily concerned with negotiations between Hussein and the British government, it also discusses the background which puts the rivalry between Hussein and Ibn Saud into context.

287 **In the Anglo-Arab labyrinth: the McMahon-Husayn correspondence and its interpretations, 1914-1939.**
Elie Kedourie.   London: Cambridge University Press, 1976.
330p. bibliog.

This book deals in depth with the negotiations between the British government and Hussein leading up to the Arab revolt, and the consequences of the negotiations and other subsequent agreements. The rivalry between Hussein and Ibn Saud is featured as part of the period leading up to the Arab revolt and of the early 1920s.

288 **Foundations of British policy in the Arab world: the Cairo Conference of 1921.**
Aaron S. Klieman.   Baltimore, Maryland; London: Johns
Hopkins Press, 1970. 322p. maps. bibliog.

Probably the best account and interpretation of the Cairo Conference, its background, deliberations, recommendations and effects. Although not strictly concerned with Saudi Arabia, it set the contemporary political pattern for the surrounding areas, and is therefore of importance to a study of this period of Saudi Arabian history.

289 **The secret lives of Lawrence of Arabia.**
Phillip Knightley, Colin Simpson.   London: Nelson; New
York: McGraw-Hill, 1969. 293p. maps. bibliog.

This biography of Lawrence broke new ground when it appeared because of the access to new material released to the Public Record Office, and to Lawrence's private papers in the Bodleian Library. The authors deal with the rivalry between Hussein and Ibn Saud in the light of Lawrence's relations with the Sherifian family during the Arab revolt, and with the India Office which had financed Ibn Saud. Also discussed are the implications of the Cairo Conference which agreed to continue paying a subsidy to Ibn Saud, but which also decided to continue support for Hussein, to recognize Abdullah in Transjordan, and Faisal as King of Iraq. This situation merely aggravated the situation as far as Ibn Saud was concerned, as he saw himself being surrounded by enemies. The result was a series of border disputes and the invasion of the Hedjaz by the Ikhwan.

290 **Secret despatches from Arabia.**

Thomas Edward Lawrence. London: Golden Cockerel Press, 1939. 173p.

A collection of articles written by Lawrence for the *Arab Bulletin* between 1916 and 1918. Not all are relevant here, but the following are valuable for a study of the relationship between the Hashemites and Ibn Saud: XXVI. The Sherif and his neighbours; XXXII. Abdullah and the Ikhwan; XXXIII. Ikhwan converts; XXXVI. Report on Khurma.

291 **Secrets of the war on Mecca.**

Thomas Edward Lawrence. *Daily Express* (London), (28 May 1920).

An article dealing with the conflict between Hussein and Ibn Saud, which Lawrence felt was irreconcilable because of the religious implications and because a solution would 'involve that most difficult thing, agreement between three government departments'.

292 **Ibn Saud and the future of Arabia.**

C. C. Lewis. *International Affairs*, vol. 12, pt. 4 (1933), p. 518-34.

The first part of this article deals with the rivalry between Ibn Saud and the Hashemite rulers of the Hedjaz and the incorporation, by force of arms, of the area into Ibn Saud's country. Although part of the conflict can be attributed to the hatred between Ibn Saud and the Hashemites, the invasion of the Hedjaz was not directly a result of this, but of the claim of Hussein to the caliphate. This action by Hussein caused a storm of hatred amongst the Wahhabis and this 'could have been controlled by no human force and the Hashemites disappeared from the holy places of Islam, regretted by none, save the Sherifs'. The second and major part of the article deals with the internal consolidation of Ibn Saud's position as ruler of the Nejd, and its evolution into the kingdom of Saudi Arabia, dealing initially with the internal power problems created by the influence of the Ikhwan. Also considered are the relations between Ibn Saud and Abdullah, and the problems caused by Ikhwan raids across into Transjordan, which was ruled by Abdullah with British support. However, the author felt that after Ibn Saud the whole political situation would change, as no other personality could control the various dissident tribes.

293 **Britain's moment in the Middle East, 1914-56.**

Elizabeth Monroe. London: Chatto and Windus; Baltimore, Maryland: Johns Hopkins Press, 1963. 254p. maps. bibliog.

Coverage of Saudi Arabia is limited but this work demonstrates how vital is an understanding of developments elsewhere to a study of Saudi Arabia. This work deals with the position of Saudi Arabia up to the outbreak of war, the rivalry between Hussein and Ibn Saud, the creation of the kingdom of Saudi Arabia, the discovery of oil, and the problems of defining frontiers. The earlier part of the book is mainly concentrated on British plans in the area in relation to the war with Germany and Turkey.

294 The Hashemite kings.
James Morris.   London: Faber, 1959. 231p. bibliog.

A biography of the Hashemite family which is relevant to a study of the relations between the Sherifians and Ibn Saud. This is seen in relation to the period prior to the Arab revolt, the effects of the peace settlement, attempts to place Hussein's sons on the thrones of Iraq and Syria, and finally in relation to the invasion of the Hedjaz and the installation of Abdullah as Amir of Transjordan.

295 T. E. Lawrence: an Arab view.
Suleiman Mousa.   London, New York: Oxford University Press, 1966. 301p. bibliog.

The relevance of this work is mainly in the area of the rivalry between Ibn Saud and Ibn Rashid prior to the outbreak of the Arab revolt, and the rivalry between Ibn Saud and the Sherifians following the peace conference. The work is important because it presents an Arab view of T. E. Lawrence and the whole question of the Arab revolt.

296 Britain, France and the Arab Middle East, 1914-20.
Jukka Nevakivi.   London: Athlone Press; Atlantic Highlands, New Jersey: Humanities Press, 1969. 284p. maps. bibliog.

This book deals primarily with Anglo-French relations during the First World War, and in particular with the political aspirations of the two nations regarding the postwar settlement. The early part of the book does, however, make a study of Britain's relations with Ibn Saud prior to the outbreak of war, and of postwar friction between Hussein and Ibn Saud.

297 The recent history of the Hedjaz.
H. St. John B. Philby.   *Journal of the Royal Central Asian Society*, vol. 12 (July 1925), p. 332-48.

The rivalry between Hussein and Ibn Saud and the invasion of the Hedjaz are dealt with and, as one would expect, the treatment is sympathetic to the claims of Ibn Saud.

298 The struggle for power in Moslem Asia.
E. Alexander Powell.   London: John Long, 1925. 320p. maps.

Discusses the problems in the Middle East following the peace settlement. Relevant for the rivalry between Hussein and Ibn Saud, and the general political developments throughout the region.

299 The holy cities of Arabia.
Eldon Rutter.   London: Putnam, 1928. 2 vols. Reprinted, 1930, in 1 vol.

An account of a trip to Mecca and Medina made immediately after the two cities had been taken from the Sherifians by the Ikhwan.

300 A prince of Arabia: the Emir Sherreef Ali Haider.
George Marquis Stewart Stitt. London: Allen & Unwin, 1948. 314p. bibliog.

Ali Haider was recognized by the Turks as Sherif of Mecca after Hussein had proclaimed the Arab revolt, but was never able to establish his authority. Valuable for the extracts from the Emir's diaries, and also for the insight into the political intrigues of the period.

301 Orientations.
Sir Ronald Storrs. London: Nicholson & Watson, 1937. 557p. maps.

Although this does not deal directly with the conflict between Hussein and Ibn Saud, it does discuss the reasons for Hussein's downfall, and the withdrawal of British support, which exposed Hussein to the attention of Ibn Saud.

302 Documents on British foreign policy, 1919-1939. First Series. Vol. IV. 1919.
Edited by E. L. Woodward, Rohan Butler. London: H.M. Stationery Office, 1952. xciii+1278p. maps.

The main interest lies in the section dealing with relations between Britain and Hussein, and between Hussein and Ibn Saud.

March arabesque.
See item no. 31.

Lord of Arabia: Ibn Saud, an intimate study of a king.
See item no. 193.

The birth of Saudi Arabia: Britain and the rise of the house of Sa'ud.
See item no. 215.

Arabian days.
See item no. 217.

The anatomy of the Saudi revolution.
See item no. 222.

Arabia and Islam.
See item no. 243.

Arabia and the Arabs.
See item no. 254.

Correspondence between Sir Henry McMahon, His Majesty's Commissioner at Cairo, and the Sherif Hussein of Mecca, July 1915-March 1916, with map.
See item no. 255.

Arabia of the Wahhabis.
See item no. 263.

Arabia today.
See item no. 264.

The emergence of the Middle East, 1914-1924.
See item no. 266.

The Arab lands, 1918-1948.
See item no. 269.

Internal consolidation

303 **Imperialism and nationalism in the fertile crescent: sources and prospects of the Arab-Israeli conflict.**
Richard Allen.   London, New York: Oxford University Press, 1974. 686p. maps. bibliog.
This book ranges much more widely than Saudi Arabia, dealing mainly with the question of Palestine and the Arabs, but in relation to the decisive role played in the fate of the Middle East by the great powers. In dealing with Saudi Arabia, apart from a brief reference to the conquest of the Hedjaz, the book mainly concentrates on the early problems relating to Palestine, the creation of Israel, and her role in Arab affairs, such as the civil war in the Yemen. The book also deals briefly with the role of Saudi Arabia in the Arab-Israeli wars and, in particular, with the use of oil as an economic and political weapon.

304 **In unknown Arabia.**
R. E. Cheesman.   London: Macmillan, 1926. 447p. map.
An account of Saudi Arabia following the incorporation of the Hedjaz into the Nejd.

305 **Arabia and the future.**
Gerald De Gaury.   *Journal of the Royal Central Asian Society*, vol. 31, pt. 1 (1944), p. 40-7. map.
An examination of the revival of the influence of the Arabian peninsula, after a period of stagnation, brought about by the progress in world communications, the internal security of Saudi Arabia, and the discovery of good quality oil in large quantities.

306 **Ibn Saud builds an empire.**
Grayson L. Kirk.   *Current History*, vol. 41, pt. 4 (1934), p. 291-7.
A consideration of the creation of the kingdom of Saudi Arabia, beginning with the rise of the Saud family, and the links forged with the Wahhabi movement. The article discusses the rivalries between Hussein and Ibn Saud, and Ibn Rashid and Ibn Saud, the results of which were victories for Ibn Saud, the addition of territory to the Nejd, and the establishment of the present kingdom of Saudi Arabia.

307 **A history of nationalism in the East.**
Hans Kohn. London: Routledge, 1929. 476p. bibliog.
Reprinted, Saint Clare Shores, Maryland: Scholarly Press (BCL
History Reprint Series).

Although dated this is an extremely valuable study, with a comparison between
nationalism in Arabia and nationalism in Turkey or Syria. The religious-based nationalism of Ibn Saud is considered to be an example of nationalism in the primitive
phase, but one which was destined to advance to full maturity.

308 **The golden jubilee in Saudi Arabia.**
H. St. John B. Philby. *Journal of the Royal Central Asian
Society*, vol. 37, pt. 2 (1956), p. 112-23. map.

An address given by the author in honour of the Saudi Arabian golden jubilee, in
which he gives a résumé of the reign of Ibn Saud and the progress made under his
rule.

309 **Jauf and the North Arabian desert.**
H. St. John B. Philby. *Geographical Journal*, vol. 62 (1923),
p. 251-9. map.

An account of a journey made to investigate the political situation at Jauf, which had
come under the control of Ibn Saud in 1921.

310 **The new reign in Saudi Arabia.**
H. St. John B. Philby. *Foreign Affairs*, vol. 32, pt. 3 (1954),
p. 446-58.

An account of the problems faced by Ibn Saud when he inherited power and set about
the establishment of a unified kingdom, cementing the Hedjaz into the Nejd, and
controlling the power of the Ikhwan.

Arabian days.
See item no. 217.

The anatomy of the Saudi revolution.
See item no. 222.

Arabia today.
See item no. 264.

The foundation of the League of Arab States.
See item no. 282.

Ibn Saud and the future of Arabia.
See item no. 292.

Oil, power and politics: conflict in Arabia, the Red Sea and the Gulf.
See item no. 311.

A house built on sand: a political economy of Saudi Arabia.
See item no. 447.

Saudi Arabia as an Arab power

311 Oil, power and politics: conflict in Arabia, the Red Sea and the Gulf.
Mordechai Abir.   London: Cass; Forest Grove, Oregon: International Scholarly Book Services, 1974. 221p. maps. bibliog.

The first chapter of this work deals with relations between Saudi Arabia and the remainder of the Gulf states before and after the British withdrawal from the area. While Saudi Arabia opposed the British presence in the Gulf and the setting up of the independent Gulf states, this attitude was changed due to Iranian pressure to preserve stability in the area, the influence of Egypt, and the refusal by America to assume the British role. The latter part of the work also considers the relations between Saudi Arabia and the Sultanate of Oman, and particularly Saudi Arabia's role in the Yemen civil war.

312 Agreement for the delimination of boundaries between Jordan and Saudi Arabia.
Middle East Journal, vol. 22, pt. 3 (1968), p. 346-9. map.

A document announcing the agreement of boundaries between Jordan and Saudi Arabia concluded between 7 July and 9 August 1965. Also reproduced is a map detailing the agreed boundaries.

313 A note on the Kuwait-Saudi Arabia neutral zone agreement of July 7 1965, relating to the partition of the zone.
Husain M. al-Bahama.   *International Comparative Law Quarterly*, vol. 17 (1968), p. 730-5.

An examination of two conflicting viewpoints expressed on the interpretation of this agreement (see articles below by J. Y. Brinton and M. T. el-Ghoneimy). According to el-Ghoneimy, the agreement was little more than an administrative device, and this note supports such an interpretation of the agreement.

314 Saudi Arabia: greatness thrust upon them.
James M. Bedore.   *Middle East International*, (Jan. 1978), p. 14-16.

The author considers the position of Saudi Arabia as an Arab power with increasing influence in the Middle East, and as a significant factor in the search for a Middle East settlement. The change in Saudi Arabia has been so rapid that the author feels that 'human history may not record another example of power acquired so fast by an élite and bureaucracy so ill-prepared to cope with the responsibilities that oil and money have suddenly brought the Kingdom'.

315 The Saudi-Kuwaiti neutral zone.
J. Y. Brinton.   *International Comparative Law Quarterly*, vol. 16 (July 1967), p. 820-3.

A criticism of the article by M. T. el-Ghoneimy which appeared in the July 1966 issue of this periodical (see below); the author argues that the contention that the partition was purely administrative was ill-founded. The author maintains that the agreement was a definite partition of an area over which, by long occupation, the two countries had exercised a joint and undisputed sovereignty. A response from el-Ghoneimy further arguing his case is also printed.

316 **The Saudi Arabia-Kuwait neutral zone.**
Edward Hoagland Brown. Beirut: Middle East Research and Publishing Centre, 1963. 150p. (Middle East Oil Monograph, no. 4).

This work deals with the question of the neutral zone in relation to the problem of the exploitation of the oil, and the shared solution reached by the two countries.

317 **Shah of Iran concerned over Saudi Arabia's future - traditional Arab régimes on the Gulf face years of crisis and turmoil.**
Alvin J. Cottrell. *New Middle East*, (31 April 1971), p. 21-3.

This article discusses the political implications of Britain's withdrawal from the Gulf, and Iranian plans to fill the power vacuum. In the report of an interview with the Shah, topics covered include the problem of the survival, or otherwise, of the traditional rulers in the Gulf States, and the attitude of Saudi Arabia toward the situation.

318 **Saudi Arabia's dilemma.**
Tom Dammann. *Interplay*, vol. 3 (Sept. 1970), p. 16-19.

An interview with King Faisal concerning Saudi Arabia's role as an Arab power. Topics covered are the question of Israel, the future after Faisal, the impact of the modern world, the problem of the Palestine liberation groups, and relations with Iraq.

319 **Saudi Arabia: next in line for revolution?**
T. Desjardins. *Atlas*, vol. 19, pt. 9 (1970), p. 30-4.

A discussion of the political situation in Saudi Arabia, and the possibility of the instability of other parts of the Arab world spreading to Saudi Arabia.

320 **Kuwait and her neighbours.**
Harold R. P. Dickson. London: Allen & Unwin, 1956. 672p.

A first-hand account of Saudi-Kuwaiti problems, and the negotiations leading to the signing of the Treaty of Muhamman and 'Uqair Protocols.

321 **The Middle East: nations, superpowers and wars.**
Yair Evron. London: Elek; New York: Praeger, 1973. 248p. bibliog.

This book is mainly concerned with the Arab-Israeli conflict, and Saudi Arabia is considered in relation to this subject in its wider context, such as its relations with Egypt in the 1950s and 1960s. Also dealt with are the inter-Arab rivalries in the remainder of the region, and specifically Saudi-Egyptian conflict in the Red Sea area, which was brought to a climax by Egyptian involvement in the Yemen civil war. However, the subsequent withdrawal of Egyptian forces from the Yemen took some of the heat out of the conflict.

322 **Arabia: when Britain goes.**

Fabian Society. London: Fabian Research Series, 1967. 28p. (No. 259).

Discusses the likely political outcome of Britain's withdrawal from the Gulf area.

323 **Faisal's Arabian alternative.**

J. Gaspard. *New Middle East*, vol. 6, pt. 1 (1969), p. 15-19.

An examination of the conflicts in the Arabian peninsula and, in particular, Saudi Arabia's policies with regard to the problems of the Arab-Israeli question, and the Arab rivalry in the Yemen. These conflicts are seen as part of the struggle for the leadership of the Arab world and control of oil production.

324 **The legal status of the Saudi-Kuwaiti neutral zone.**

Mohamed Talaat el-Ghoneimy. *International Comparative Law Quarterly*, vol. 15 (1966), p. 690-717.

An extremely detailed examination of the neutral zone which the author considers special and possibly unique, but little written about from the legal viewpoint. The article is in three parts. The first reviews the historical background, dealing with the emergence of Kuwait and Saudi Arabia and the creation of the neutral zone. The second part deals with the problems of boundaries on the northern maritime border, the territorial waters and the Qam and Umm el Maradim islands. Finally the article deals with the international legal status of the zone, which the author believes can be defined as neutral in the sense that it is not national, i.e. 'it does not belong to one state but belongs to two partners'.

325 **From slumber to riches: an Arabian dream.**

Robert Graham. *New Middle East*, nos. 52-53 (Jan.-Feb. 1973), p. 16-18.

A consideration of the effects that the oil wealth of Saudi Arabia will have on the country's regional and global role. These effects are to be seen in relation to Saudi Arabia's dealings with her Arab neighbours, the whole question of Israel and Palestine, and the utilization of the income from oil in the international economy. On the basis of this the writer concludes that 'it seems a fairly safe assumption that Saudi Arabia from now on will demand greater attention, not only in the Arab world but in the industrialized countries as well'.

326 **United Kingdom memorial: arbitration concerning Buraimi and the common frontier between Abu Dhabi and Saudi Arabia.**

Great Britain. Foreign Office. London: H.M. Stationery Office, 1955.

Although the arbitration proceedings of 1955 were abortive, this account presents a valuable assessment of the difficulties that lay in the way of a settlement of the territorial dispute between the two states and, to a lesser extent, Oman. It is also useful for an account of Wahhabi history and Anglo-Saudi relations. See also the Saudi Arabian government's memorial on the subject (item no. 369).

327 Jordan-Saudi border demarcation.

W. E. Greenip. *Viewpoints*, vol. 6, pt. 1 (1966), p. 24.

An outline of the agreement settling the disputed border between the two countries.

328 Arabia without sultans.

Fred Halliday. London: Penguin, 1974; New York: Random House, 1975. 527p. map.

This work deals with political unrest in Arabia, particularly with the revolts in the Dhofar region of Oman and the Yemeni civil war. Chapter 2 deals exclusively with Saudi Arabia, concentrating on the development of the state, and the opposition to the régime which was crushed by the Saudi authorities. Also considered is the civil war in the Yemen, which led to Egypt and Saudi Arabia being involved on opposing sides. The book aims at showing the state of the working class in the authoritarian régimes of Arabia, the divisions in Arabian society, and the capitalist influence in the economics and politics of the Arabian peninsula.

329 Saudi Arabia: bonanza and repression.

Fred Halliday. *New Left Review*, no. 68 (1973), p. 3-26.

An article contrasting the economic boom in Saudi Arabia with the lack of democratic institutions, autocratic rule, and the accumulation of wealth by the ruling minority.

330 Arab attitudes to Israel.

Yehoshafat Harkabi. London: Vallentine Mitchell, 1973; New Brunswick, New Jersey: Transaction Books, 1974. 527p.

A very detailed analysis of Arab attitudes to Israel using extracts from books, the press and radio, to illustrate the explicit aims and their ideological explanation in the roots of the Palestinian problem. References to Saudi Arabia appear throughout the text but the selection presents only one side of the case.

331 Information and the Arab cause.

M. Abdel-Kader Hatem. London, New York: Longman, 1974. 336p.

Saudi Arabia is dealt with here as part of the Middle East, and of the Arab cause, with regard to Israel and the problem of Palestine. Although mainly concerned with the problem of conflict in the Middle East, this is an important work because of its consideration of the effects of public relations, propaganda and the media as a significant factor in the shaping of opinion about the Arab world.

332 The road to Ramadan.

Mohamed Heikal. London: Collins; New York: Quadrangle, 1975. 285p.

An account of the Arab preparations for the October War, 1973, by the former editor of *Al Ahram*. As regards Saudi Arabia the aspects covered are the relations between Saudi Arabia and the states which directly confront Israel, and the use of oil as a political weapon. weapon.

333 The war of atonement, October 1973.
Chaim Herzog. London: Weidenfeld & Nicolson; Boston, Massachusetts: Little, Brown, 1975. 300p. maps.

An account of the events leading up to and the course of the 1973 war, from its roots back in the Six-Day War. The book deals in places with the role of Saudi Arabia in Arab-Israeli relations.

334 The Saudis look to Washington.
David Holden. *Middle East International*, no. 72 (June 1977), p. 4-6.

The author examines the relationship between Saudi Arabia and America, which is a significant factor in dealings between the major Arab governments and America. This relationship is also economic in that Saudi Arabia supplies 40 per cent of American oil imports, as well as those of her allies, and is a large investor in the American capital market, as well as a large importer of American goods and services.

335 Nationalism in the Middle East.
Harry N. Howard. *Orbis*, vol. 10, pt. 4 (1964), p. 1200-13.

A discussion of the emergence of nationalism in the Middle East following the break-up of the Ottoman empire. It is clear that in Saudi Arabia's case the process was different from that which applied to other countries such as Syria. The point is made, however, that nationalism has and will have an effect on the structure of Saudi Arabian society, as will technological advances. The only certain thing is that 'the Arab world will be restless and unsettled, sometimes at strife with itself and with us, while its people strive to find their way through the maze which leads from a medieval past to a modern future'.

336 Iran-Saudi Arabia: agreement concerning sovereignty over al-Arabiyah and Farsi islands and delimination of submarine boundaries.
International Legal Materials, vol. 8, pt. 3 (1969), p. 493-6.

The text of the agreement.

337 Revolutionary transformation in the Arab world: Habash and his comrades from nationalism to Marxism.
Walid Kazziha. London: Knight; New York: St. Martin's Press, 1975. 118p. bibliog.

This work examines the growth of the Arab nationalist movement following the Palestine War of 1948. Initial attempts to establish a base for the movement in Saudi Arabia petered out for lack of support, though it did recruit student members from the American University of Beirut. The author considers the growth of the movement in the Arabian peninsula in the various countries in which it had either secured actual support or financial backing. However, the Arab defeat in 1967 caused its disintegration into a series of scattered groups and factions, which became Marxist-oriented and therefore opposed by the Saudi Arabian government.

338 The Arabian peninsula in Arab and power politics.
A. R. Kelidar. In: *The Arabian peninsula: society and politics.* Edited by Derek Hopwood. London: Allen & Unwin; Lotowa, New Jersey: Rowman & Littlefield, 1972, p. 145-59.

This essay deals with the relations between the various Arab states and, in this connection, the question of Saudi Arabia's relations with her neighbouring states is considered.

339 The Buraimi oasis dispute.
John B. Kelly. *International Affairs,* vol. 32, pt. 3 (1956), p. 318-26.

An account of the dispute between Saudi Arabia on the one hand, and the Sultan of Oman and the Sheikh of Abu Dhabi on the other, over the Buraimi oasis, with Britain acting on behalf of the latter parties in their dealings with Saudi Arabia. The author, an expert on the political aspects of the Gulf area, deals with the historical background to the dispute, the significance of the oasis, and the contemporary events leading to the reawakening of the dispute. The article also points to the danger that the dispute, and others of a similar nature, could be regarded as a pursuit of Western interests by Britain, whereas the historical background proves otherwise, but the fault for any such misunderstandings 'would seem to lie partly with the British government for not making the history of the case more widely known'.

340 Eastern Arabian frontiers.
John B. Kelly. London: Faber; New York, Fernhill House, 1964. 319p. maps.

An important book for understanding the problem of the disputed eastern frontiers of Saudi Arabia, which was a continuation of Saudi Arabia's dispute with the littoral states, who sought to preserve their independence in the face of Saudi expansion. The author traces the history of Saudi expansion in eastern Arabia, and the cause of various negotiations regarding frontiers. The second part of the book deals with post-Second World War events, especially the Buraimi oasis dispute 1952-55, and the various claims and counter-claims.

341 The future in Arabia.
John B. Kelly. *International Affairs,* vol. 42, pt. 4 (1966), p. 619-40.

A great deal of this article is outside the scope of this bibliography as it is concerned with the whole of the Arabian peninsula, and constitutes an attempt to predict future developments in the area. In the context of Saudi Arabia consideration is given to the possibility of a revolution against the Saudi ruling house. The author argues that the monarchical system is the only workable system of government for Saudi Arabia in the foreseeable future. In addition, those that argue in favour of the country being ripe for revolution 'underestimate the staying power of the Saudi royal house, its grip upon its people, and the tribal and regional bases of its strength'. Saudi Arabia's position is also considered in relation to Kuwait, where the author sees the Saudi government being unable to stand by and acquiesce in either Egyptian or Iraqi occupation.

342 Sovereignty and jurisdiction in eastern Arabia.
John B. Kelly. *International Affairs*, vol. 34, pt. 1 (1958), p. 16-24.

A further consideration, by an expert in the field, of the various problems of spheres of influence and frontiers in eastern Arabia which involve Saudi Arabia. The three disputes can best be summarized as follows: 1. Between Saudi Arabia and Abu Dhabi over the coast and hinterland between Zator and Abu Dhabi town; 2. Between Saudi Arabia and the Sultanate of Oman and Abu Dhabi over the Buraimi oasis; 3. Between Saudi Arabia and Qatar over their common frontier. In essence, claims to disputed territories are based upon one or both of two grounds: past or present occupation, or current exercise of jurisdiction. The article examines each of the disputes in question from those standpoints and points out that until they are solved 'King Saud will continue to feel free to challenge the authority of the Sultan of Muscat and Oman and that of the rulers of the Trucial shaikhdoms in the western marches of their dominions'.

343 Kingdom of the keys.
The Economist, vol. 257 (4 Oct. 1975), p. 13.

A consideration of Saudi Arabia's key role in the Middle East due to her proven oil reserves. Her role is particularly crucial in relation to Egypt's attempts to secure peace in the area, as the latter's economy is heavily dependent upon Saudi Arabian subsidy.

344 Confrontation: the Middle East war and world politics.
Walter Laqueur. London: Wildwood House; New York: Quadrangle, 1974. 245p. maps.

This work is primarily concerned with the Arab-Israeli War of 1973 and its wider implications through the use of oil as a political weapon. In dealing with Saudi Arabia the work considers the rapprochement with Egypt, relations with Jordan, and the power situation in the Middle East. The use of the oil weapon is also considered in terms of relations with the United States, and the role of Saudi Arabia in the acceptance of a peace formula.

345 Riyadh and Washington: a mutual reliance.
Abdul Lateef. *Middle East International*, (July 1978), p. 16-18.

Discusses the relationship between Saudi Arabia and America, based on the importance of oil, and the significance of Saudi Arabia as a counter to Soviet and communist influence in the Middle East.

346 The Persian Gulf in the twentieth century.
John Marlowe. London: Cresset Press, 1962. 278p. maps. bibliog.

Although this book is concerned with the whole of the Gulf region, Saudi Arabia is mentioned throughout, and the whole forms an important contribution to an understanding of the contemporary history of the area. A considerable proportion of the text is concerned with the question of oil, but among other topics considered are the various border disputes, relations with Egypt and Iran, and the rise of Arab nationalism in the Gulf.

347 **Boundaries and petroleum in southern Arabia.**
Alexander Melamid. *Geographical Review*, vol. 47, pt. 4 (1957), p. 589-91.

Discusses the complex situation regarding exploration and the granting of oil concessions, in the light of border disputes between the Yemen and Saudi Arabia, Oman and Saudi Arabia, and Kuwait and Saudi Arabia.

348 **The Buraimi oasis dispute.**
Alexander Melamid. *Middle East Affairs*, vol. 7 (1956), p. 56-63. map.

This dispute was a complex problem involving Saudi Arabia, Abu Dhabi and Oman and the United Kingdom, which at that time still had a presence in the Gulf States and Oman, with responsibility for foreign relations. This article explains the somewhat involved background to the dispute, which in 1956 was due to go to arbitration because of the presence of water, without which tribes on either side could not survive, and because of the possible presence of oil-bearing strata.

349 **The economic geography of neutral territories.**
Alexander Melamid. *Geographical Review*, vol. 45, pt. 3 (1955), p. 359-74.

Discusses the question of whether economic growth affects the status of neutral territories or vice versa. Problems related to the Middle East, i.e. the Saudi-Kuwaiti neutral zone, and the then unresolved Buraimi dispute, are discussed on p. 363-9.

350 **Geographical boundaries and nomadic grazing.**
Alexander Melamid. *Geographical Review*, vol. 55, pt. 2 (1965), p. 287-90.

A discussion of the problem of geographical boundaries, which have become important in Arabia because of oil, in relation to the traditional areas of tribal influence as defined by the use of grazing rights. This aspect has caused conflict in the drawing up of political boundaries between Saudi Arabia and her Gulf neighbours.

351 **Oil and the evolution of boundaries in eastern Arabia.**
Alexander Melamid. *Geographical Review*, vol. 44, pt. 2 (1954), p. 295-6.

A consideration of the Buraimi oasis dispute.

352 **The political geography of the Gulf of Aqaba.**
Alexander Melamid. *Annals of the Association of American Geographers*, vol. 47, pt. 3 (1957), p. 231-40.

A consideration of the strategic and economic importance of the Gulf as an international waterway.

353 The United States and Saudi Arabia: a policy analysis.
Emile A. Nakhleh. Washington, D.C.: American Enterprise Institute, 1975. 69p. map.

An examination of relationships between Saudi Arabia and the United States, analysing the changes taking place within Saudi Arabia and the effect that these changes have on the determining of Saudi Arabian policy.

354 U.S. postures in West Asia: defence arrangements with Saudi Arabia - a case study.
R. Narajan. *Studies in Politics: National and International*, (1971), p. 298-323.

Discusses the two countries' mutual reliance in relation to Middle East affairs as a region, and in relations with the Soviet Union.

355 Arab guerilla power, 1967-1972.
Edgar O'Ballance. London: Faber; Hamden, Connecticut: Shoe String Press, 1974. 246p. maps.

This work is mainly concerned with the aftermath of the 1967 war and the guerilla activities of the Palestinian Arabs. References are made to Saudi Arabia throughout the text, though her involvement in this subject is minimal.

356 Saudi Arabia's wealth: a two-edged sword.
Malcolm Peck. *New Middle East*, (Jan. 1972), p. 5-7.

A further examination of the role of Saudi Arabia as an Arab power, following the power vacuum created by Britain's withdrawal from the Gulf, and her recognition of the United Arab Emirates and the Sultanate of Oman. An examination is also made of the theological hostility towards Zionism, manifested in economic support for Egypt and Jordan, and relations with the larger Islamic world. Growing affluence and oil reserves account for Saudi Arabia's importance and although this 'may be a two-edged sword for a traditional monarchy', creating social and political instability, 'it can also be made a solvent of dissidence and opposition'.

357 Arabia in retrospect.
H. St. John B. Philby. *Middle East Forum*, vol. 33, pt. 1 (1958), p. 14-15.

Brief survey of the rise of Saudi Arabia.

358 Arabian jubilee.
H. St. John B. Philby. London: Hale, 1952. 280p.

This work was written to commemorate Ibn Saud's fiftieth anniversary as a ruler, and is a record of the changes that were brought about during his reign and the problems associated with these changes. Philby also deals with his own personal relationship with the royal family, and, in particular, the conflicts and clashes that had taken place.

359 The Arab world today.

H. St. John B. Philby. *London Quarterly World Affairs* (July 1945), p. 124-30.

This article discusses the problems to be faced in the Middle East following the end of the Second World War. In his analysis the author refers back to the question of the Sykes-Picot agreement and the Cairo Conference of 1921. The Arab League was established in 1945, and this is seen as significant as it will serve as 'a valuable outlet for the canalization and dissemination of Arab sentiment in respect of all matters affecting the Arabs as a whole'.

360 Britain and Arabia.

H. St. John B. Philby. *Nineteenth Century and After*, vol. 117 (1935), p. 574-7.

361 A pilgrim in Arabia.

H. St. John B. Philby. London: Hale, 1946. 198p.

The main thread of this book, written immediately after the end of the Second World War, is the desire of the Arab nations for independence. Also considered is the form of government and administration in Saudi Arabia, which the author feels is not adequate to cope with the pressures of the modern world. The pilgrimage is also dealt with in detail, and Philby provides a good account of the pilgrimage and the problems presented by the influx of pilgrims placing so great a strain on resources.

362 The trouble in Arabia: Iraq and Najd frontier.

H. St. John B. Philby. *Contemporary Review*, vol. 41 (1928), p. 705-8.

Discusses the problems of defining the frontier between the two countries, especially in the light of strained relations.

363 The politics of Palestinian nationalism.

W. B. Quandt, F. Jabber, A. M. Lesch. Berkeley, California; London: University of California Press, 1973. 234p. maps. bibliog.

This book deals with the evolution and politics of Palestinian nationalism, particularly with regard to the position of the Arab states, including Saudi Arabia. It considers the role of Saudi Arabia as a mediator between the Palestine Liberation Organization and Jordan, and as a supporter for the Palestinian cause. Also considered are relations with Egypt, which reached a low with both countries' involvement in the Yemen civil war during the 1960s.

364 The Buraimi dispute, the British armed aggression.

A. S. Sahwell. *Islamic Review*, vol. 44 (April 1956), p. 13-17.

The Saudi case for the claim to the Buraimi oasis, which was disputed between Saudi Arabia, Abu Dhabi and Oman. The other claimants to the oasis were represented by Britain who, at that time, was responsible for handling foreign affairs on their behalf.

365 **The arms bazaar.**

Anthony Sampson. London: Hodder & Stoughton, 1977. 352p.

Although primarily a book about the expansion of the armaments companies, the men who control them, and their methods of business, there is considerable coverage of the Middle East, because this area is a growth market. The author deals with Saudi Arabia's demand for sophisticated arms, to be paid for by increasingly large oil revenues, and the support to poorer Arab states in the form of finance and arms. Also dealt with are the rivalry between the arms companies and the various governments to secure contracts, and the problem of supplying expatriate labour to maintain the equipment once sold.

366 **Ibn Saud's program for Arabia.**

Richard H. Sanger. *Middle East Journal*, vol. 1 (1947), p. 180-90.

An account of Ibn Saud's plans for the modernization and economic development of Saudi Arabia.

367 **Saudi Arabia and South Yemen's border clash: its background and implications.**

Arab World, (27 March 1973), p. 11-12.

368 **Saudi Arabia: focus on the eastern provinces.**

The Times (London), (21 Nov. 1977), 10p.

A special report dealing with the eastern province, with its oil wealth, natural gas and port facilities. Also considered are agricultural and rural electrification, improvements to transportation and communications, and the problem of manpower needs.

369 **Arbitration for the settlement of the territorial dispute between Muscat and Abu Dhabi on one side and Saudi Arabia on the other: memorial of the government of Saudi Arabia.**

Saudi Arabia. Government. Cairo: al-Maaref Press, 1955. 3 vols. maps.

The Saudi Arabian memorial, which should be read in conjunction with that issued by the British Foreign Office (see earlier in this section under Great Britain. Foreign Office).

370 **Saudi Arabia: what happens after Faisal?**

Foreign Report, no. 1225 (1971), p. 4-5.

Speculation as to the future position of Saudi Arabia, and the internal situation after the rule of Faisal.

371 **King Faisal's first year.**
Victor Sheean. *Foreign Affairs*, vol. 44, pt. 2 (1966), p. 304-13.

An account of Faisal's first year as ruler of Saudi Arabia, by his future biographer.

372 **Arab nationalism: a study in political geography.**
C. G. Smith. *Geography* , vol. 43 (1958), p. 229-42.

This article concentrates on the post-First World War period and considers the Middle East in the light of political geography. Saudi Arabia is dealt with as part of the overall situation, and within the context of moves towards union and co-operation between Arab countries.

373 **Saudi Arabia in international politics.**
Robert R. Sullivan. *Review of Politics*, vol. 32, pt. 4 (Oct. 1970), p. 436-60.

The author draws comparisons between the policy of Saudi Arabia prior to and after 1962, which is seen as a watershed date. The author argues that the policy was inconsistent prior to 1962, and this view is examined in relation to the various border disputes with Kuwait, Abu Dhabi and Oman. After 1962 the author sees a consistent approach to foreign policy, an approach which can broadly be defined as that of a powerful conservative power in conflict with radical outside powers.

374 **National security challenge to Saudi Arabia.**
Dale R. Tahtinen. Washington, D.C.: American Enterprise Institute, 1974. 49p.

A discussion of the potential conflicts facing Saudi Arabia during the next decade. The booklet discusses the arrangements for defence and assesses the capability and effectiveness of the facilities.

375 **Middle East: tricontinental hub, a strategic survey.**
United States. Department of the Army. Washington, D.C.: Dept. of the Army, 1965. 167p (Pamphlet 550-2).

Considers the geo-political situation in the light of American interests and policy.

376 **Jordan - Saudi Arabia.**
United States. Department of State. Bureau of Intelligence. Washington, D.C.: Department of State, 1965. (Boundary Studies Series, no. 60).

In the same series the following two volumes are also relevant: *Kuwait - Saudi Arabia*, 1971 (no. 103); *Iraq - Saudi Arabia*, 1971 (no. 111).

377 **Faces in Shem.**
D. Van der Meulen. · London: Murray, 1961. 194p.

Deals mainly with the Yemen, but of interest for relations with Saudi Arabia.

378 The foreign policy of Ibn Saud, 1936-1939.

D. C. Watt. *Journal of the Royal Central Asian Society*, vol. 50, pt. 2 (1963), p. 152-60.

This article discusses the evolution of Saudi Arabia's foreign relations, from contacts solely with Britain to a wider role in the world at large, and eventually to membership of the United Nations.

379 When an era trembles.

The Economist, no. 6866, vol. 254 (29 March 1978), p. 11-12.

An examination of the situation in Saudi Arabia, following the assassination of King Faisal, which examines the policies he followed, and the changes that might result from the enforced change of leadership.

380 Equitable solutions for offshore boundaries: the 1968 Saudi Arabia-Iran agreement.

Richard Young. *American Journal of International Law*, vol. 64, pt. 1 (1970), p. 152-7.

A comment on the agreement between the two countries, covering their respective offshore areas in the Arabian Gulf.

Saudi Arabia today: introduction to the richest oil power.
See item no. 10.

March arabesque.
See item no. 31.

The Near East: a modern history.
See item no. 73.

Arabia phoenix.
See item no. 106.

Britain and the Arabs: a study of fifty years, 1908-1958.
See item no. 200.

Arabian days.
See item no. 217.

Middle East: past and present.
See item no. 272.

The foundation of the League of Arab States.
See item no. 282.

Britain's moment in the Middle East, 1914-56.
See item no. 293.

A house built on sand: a political economy of Saudi Arabia.
See item no. 447.

Saudi Arabia 2000: a strategy for growth.
See item no. 496.

Oil and state in the Middle East.
See item no. 547.

Anthropology

381 Beyond Arabian sands; the people, places and politics of the Arab world.
G. C. Butler.   New York: Devin-Adair, 1964. 223p.

382 Caravan: the story of the Middle East.
Carleton Stevens Coon.   New York, London: Holt, Rinehart & Winston, 1965. 386p.
The classic account of the peoples and races of Arabia which, although dated, is an indispensable source of anthropological information.

383 The Bedouin.
Shirley Kay.   Newton Abbot, England: David & Charles, 1978. 159p. maps.
An examination of the Bedouin, beginning with the traditional nomadic role based on feuds and inter-tribal raiding, and discussing the changes that economic prosperity has brought about. The author also deals with the effects of education on the younger generation, and the replacement of traditional cures by modern medicine. One section is devoted to a consideration of the traditions in art and poetry, together with customs and beliefs, and the codes of honour and hospitality. The author also attempts to assess the future of the Bedouin in this changing society, and concludes that an adaptation to modern life is possible, but that there is also still a role for the nomadic stock herder, provided the right encouragement is forthcoming.

384 The Arab mind considered: a need for understanding.
John Laffin.   London: Cassell; New York: Taplinger, 1975. 180p. map.
An attempt to explain the politics and attitudes of the Arabs and the religious, linguistic and psychological influences that affect the individual Arab's outlook. The author considers the influence of history, the question of Islam, language and literature, and the structure of society; among other topics.

Anthropology

385 The manners and customs of the Rwala Bedouins.
A. Musil.   New York: American Geographical Society, 1928.
712p. (Oriental Explorations and Studies, no. 6).

386 The 'tribal' sector in Middle Eastern society: a profile.
C. A. O. van Nieuwenhuijze.   *Correspondance d'Orient Etudes*, vol. 5-6 (1964), p. 39-62.

An extremely detailed examination of the tribal sector in Middle Eastern society, not restricted by reasons of geography. It is important, in particular, for its insight into the problems faced by Western observers in trying to understand the sociocultural phenomena of the Middle East, for the character of the area 'is quite elusive; maybe even more so than in many other cultural areas....Consequently, the Western observer runs the risk of trying to gain insight...in a manner that need not be congenial to the Middle Eastern bent of mind'.

387 Nomads and nomadism in the arid zones.
International Social Science Journal, vol. 11, pt. 4 (1959), p. 539-45.

388 Anthropological measurements on the Arab Bedouin with comments on their customs.
W. Shanklin.   *Man*, no. 206, vol. 53 (1953), p. 134.

389 A survey of recent Middle Eastern ethnology.
Louise E. Sweet.   *Middle East Journal*, vol. 23 (1969), p. 221-9.

A review article of which only the section on 'nomadic pastoralists' is really of relevance here, though none of the cited works is solely concerned with Saudi Arabia.

Saudi Arabia: its people, its society, its culture.
See item no. 14.

Rub' al Khali.
See item no. 118.

Sheba's daughters: being a record of travel in southern Arabia.
See item no. 119.

Two notes from Central Arabia.
See item no. 177.

Religion

Islam

390 **Medina, second city of Islam.**
A. A. al-Ansan. *Aramco World*, vol. 15, pt. 4 (1964), p. 30-3.

An examination of the role played by Medina in the life of the Prophet and the development of Islam.

391 **King Ibn Saud: our faith and your iron.**
William A. Eddy. *Middle East Journal*, vol. 17, pt. 3 (1963), p. 257-63.

A discussion of the part played by the Islamic faith in Saudi Arabia, especially in its relations with the West. The Saudis' attitude was summed up by Ibn Saud: 'We Muslims have the one true faith, but Allah gave you the iron which is inanimate, amoral, neither prohibited nor mentioned in the Qur'an. We will use your iron but leave our faith alone'.

392 **Modern trends in Islam.**
Hamilton A. R. Gibb. Chicago, Illinois: Chicago University Press, 1947. 141p.

A valuable introduction to contemporary developments in Islam.

393 **Saudi Arabia (Islam in politics).**
J. J. Malone. *Muslim World*, vol. 56 (1966), p. 290-5.

An examination of the role played by Islam in the politics and development of Saudi Arabia. The author considers the fruitless attempts by King Faisal to achieve a grouping of Islamic states; but other attempts to arrive at a policy guided by Islam, especially with regard to Yemen, were more successful. Also considered is the part played by the Wahhabis in the early growth of Saudi Arabia, and the problems that this influence has caused in the course of attempts to introduce changes necessary to ensure modernization. 'The task may be too great. The balance may not be achieved'.

394 Saudi Arabia: the Islamic island.
G. Rentz. *Journal of International Affairs*, vol. 19, pt. 1 (1965), p. 115-25.

The author discusses the position of Saudi Arabia in relation to Islam, and the reasons for the strength of religion in Saudi society. He also deals with the effects of the income from oil on Saudi Arabian society, with reference to gradual moves towards secularization. These changes have not been without their problems, as conservative opposition to secularization has acted as a brake on social and economic development. On the other hand, 'opposition has appeared to the interference of the ulema in the daily lives of men through the prescribing of standards for almost every facet of community or individual activity'.

395 Revival and reform in Islam.
Fazlur Rohman. In: *Cambridge history of Islam. Vol. 2: The further Islamic lands; Islamic society and civilization.* London, New York: Cambridge University Press, 1971, p. 632-56.

A general study which deals in part with the Wahhabi movement and its impact on the revival of Islam.

396 The Muslim mind.
Charis Waddy. London, New York: Longman, 1976. 205p.

Although not strictly related to Saudi Arabia, this important work is included here because it is a Western interpretation of Islam and Islamic attitudes and thought. As Islam plays such an important part in Saudi Arabian life, any book which contributes to an understanding of its significance is of relevance to an appreciation of Saudi Arabia.

397 The social organization of Mecca and the origins of Islam.
E. R. Wolf. *Southwestern Journal of Anthropology*, vol. 7, pt. 4 (1951), p. 329-53.

398 Arabia: the cradle of Islam.
Samuel Marinus Zwemer. Edinburgh: Oliphant, 1900. 434p.

An account of Arabia, concentrating mainly on its significance to Islam, because of the holy cities and the Hajj.

Arabian days.
See item no. 217.

Wahhabism in Arabia, past and present.
See item no. 242.

Some social aspects of Bedouin settlements in Wadi Fatima, Saudi Arabia.
See item no. 418.

The pilgrimage - the Hajj

399 **The Hajj - the most sacred journey.**
Mohammed Amin. *Middle East,* no. 18 (1976), p. 18-21.

An account of the Hajj as a feat of logistics. The author begins by outlining the historical growth of the pilgrimage, before discussing the arrangements now necessary in order to provide accommodation, food and sanitation for the pilgrims.

400 **The Haj - importance of the annual pilgrimage to the holy places.**
N. Ashford. *Financial Times* (London), (23 June 1969).

A special report which discusses the importance to the economy of the annual Hajj.

401 **The Hijaz railway and the pilgrimage to Mecca.**
Gerald H. Blake, R. King. *Asian Affairs,* vol. 59, pt. 3 (1972), p. 317-25.

Provides first a brief background to the pilgrimage and the history of the first Hedjaz railway, discussing the raising of the capital and difficulties encountered in construction. The railway was only operational for five years before the outbreak of war in 1914, and during this period there was an upsurge in the number of pilgrims. The article then deals with the reconstruction work between 1964 and 1967, which was halted by the Arab-Israeli War of 1967, after 2,000 bridges had been rebuilt, 840 embankments repaired, and 12 miles of track laid. 'It is clear that with some £15 million invested...there are strong practical arguments for completing reconstruction. The question is now whether an economic case can be made out for a new Hijaz railway.' The authors attempt finally to answer this question by considering the prospects for freight and passenger transportation.

402 **Overseas visitors and the Hajj.**
Gerald H. Blake. *Middle East Yearbook,* (1977), p. 93-5.

A description of the importance of the Hajj to the Muslim world and to Saudi Arabia, which has to cope with the logistic problems raised by the huge influx of pilgrims.

403 **A rising tide in Mecca.**
Gerald H. Blake. *Middle East International,* no. 58 (1976), p. 16-18.

An examination of the pilgrimage to Mecca, with reference to the problems faced by the Saudi Arabian authorities in catering for pilgrims whose numbers are increasing because of improvements in communications and standards of living in other Moslem countries.

404 **The hard way to Mecca.**
Peter Boxhall. *Middle East International,* no. 62 (1976), p. 23-5.

A follow-up to 'Pilgrims across Africa' (see next item), which deals with the overland routes used by pilgrims to make the Hajj, and the problems faced by the travellers.

405 **Pilgrims across Africa.**

Peter Boxhall. *Middle East International*, no. 58 (1976), p. 18-20. map.

An account of the pilgrimage, examining the various routes across Africa adopted by the pilgrims, from the beginning of the Hajj to the present time.

406 **The pilgrim railway.**

W. Carter. *Geographical Magazine*, vol. 39, pt. 6 (1966), p. 422-33. map.

An account of the building of the Hedjaz railway, and a description of the country through which it passes. The author concentrates on the religious basis for its existence, and the plans which existed at the time of writing to reopen the line for the Hajj.

407 **Pilgrim's road.**

D. Da Cruz. *Aramco World*, vol. 16, pt. 5 (1965), p. 24-33.

Deals with the various routes used by pilgrims on the Hajj, and the order of travel within the Hajj itself.

408 **From America to Mecca: an airborne pilgrimage.**

A. S. Ghafur. *National Geographic Magazine*, vol. 104, pt. 1 (1953), p. 1-60.

An account of a modern pilgrim undertaking the Hajj.

409 **The sacred journey, being pilgrimage to Makkah: the traditions, dogma and Islamic ritual that govern the lives and the destiny of more than five hundred million who call themselves Muslim; one seventh of mankind.**

Ahmad Kamal. London: Allen & Unwin, 1964. 197p.

In English and Arabic.

410 **The pilgrimage to Mecca: some geographical and historical aspects.**

Russell King. *Erdkunde*, vol. 26 (1972), p. 61-72. maps.

A study of the pilgrimage from the geographical and historical aspects, with reference to the origins of the pilgrimage and its effects upon the transport system, and the resultant building of the Hedjaz railway which in turn produced an increase in numbers. In conclusion, the author considers the changing character of the pilgrimage, especially with regard to the various environmental improvements made to cater for the pilgrimage.

411 The Hejaz railway and the Muslim pilgrimage; a case of Ottoman political propaganda.
Muhammed 'Anf Ibn Ahmad al-Munayyir, translated by Jacob Landau. Detroit, Michigan: Wayne State University Press, 1971.

This work is, in the main, an argument in favour of the building of the Hedjaz railway, but it also contains information on the opposition of the Bedouin, who saw it as a threat to their position. Also given are accounts of the ceremonial aspects of the pilgrimage.

412 Once a year in Mecca: Saudi Arabia's six-day problem.
Gwyn Rawley, Soleiman A. el- Hamdan. *Geographical Magazine*, vol. 49, pt. 12 (1977), p. 753-9.

An examination of the Hajj and, in particular, the problems that the influx of over 700,000 pilgrims cause to the authorities as regards the provision of accommodation, medical facilities, etc. The authors deal with the procedure to be followed by the pilgrim, the modes of transportation used by the pilgrims, and the changes that have taken place over the years. The problem of the increase in numbers is also considered, especially in relation to the facilities that are required during the short period of the pilgrimage. The authors estimate that, with improvements in transportation and economic circumstances, the number of pilgrims from outside Saudi Arabia will number some 1,300,000, with another 800,000 coming from within Saudi Arabia. Because of this the Mecca region will need to receive an investment out of all proportion to the needs of the resident population. 'The problems afforded by the ever-increasing numbers of people attending the Hajj have meant that priority has had to be given to the Mecca region, while other areas have suffered accordingly.'.

413 A modern pilgrim in Mecca.
Arthur John Byng Wavell. London: Constable, 1918. 232p.

A true and faithful account of the religion and manners of the Muhammadans.
See item no. 95.

A pilgrim in Arabia.
See item no. 361.

Economic report: Saudi Arabia.
See item no. 500.

Jiddah and the western province.
See item no. 511.

Population and Social Structure

414 Population and society in the Arab East.
Gabriel Baer. London: Routledge, 1964. 275p. maps. New ed.
1977.

415 Populations of the Middle East and North Africa: a geographical approach.
J. L. Clarke, W. B. Fisher. London: University of London
Press; New York: Holmes & Meier, 1972. 432p. maps. bibliog.
A demographic study of the Middle East (including Saudi Arabia), concentrating on
the main features.

416 The Arab of the desert: a glimpse into Bedouin life in Kuwait and Saudi Arabia.
Harold R. P. Dickson. London: Allen & Unwin; New York:
Barnes & Noble, 1949. 2nd ed., 1952. 648p.
This book, with its detailed descriptions of Bedouin life in Kuwait and Saudi Arabia,
is already a classic. The author provides information about the customs, costume and
domestic utensils of the tribes, backed by detailed illustrations.

417 Trends in the components of population growth in the Arab countries of the Middle East: a survey of present information.
M. A. el-Bodry. *Demography*, vol. 2 (1965), p. 140-86.
Only the initial part of this article is relevant, as Saudi Arabia is not included in the
area surveys. In the general introduction the author makes the point that, although
there is scarcity and inaccuracy of data, some information is available through popula-

tion registers and indirect sources like housing or agricultural censuses, and this can throw light on population composition and distribution. These studies can also be used to illustrate 'external and internal migration, and levels or trends in some countries, and to study changes in these components of population change, in relation to general economic growth'.

418 Some social aspects of Bedouin settlements in Wadi Fatima, Saudi Arabia.

Motoko Katakura. *Orient* (Japan), vol. 9 (1973), p. 67-108.

A very detailed study of a significant settlement which has existed since the time of the Prophet, carried out between September 1978 and August 1970. Wadi Fatima was chosen because of its strategic importance for travel, water and agriculture. The social structure of the population is composed of complete Bedouins, semi-Bedouins, the settled Bedouins, water company employees and foreign-born residents. The community is discussed in detail under the following headings: 1. Types of population; 2. Definition of a 'village'; 3. Dwellings; 4. Religion; 5. Festivals; 6. Clothing; 7. Life cycle; 8. Medicine and superstition. The article is illustrated and contains statistical details.

419 Estimate of the rate of increase of the population of Saudi Arabia.

H. M. al-Kaylani. Beirut: American University of Beirut. Economic Research Unit, 1964.

420 Saudi Arabia: population and the making of a modern state.

R. McGregor. In: *Populations of the Middle East and North Africa: a geographical approach.* By J. L. Clarke and W. B. Fisher. London: University of London Press; New York: Holmes & Meier, 1972. 432p. maps. bibliog.

421 Bedouin life in contemporary Arabia.

C. D. Mathews. *Rivista degli Studi Orientali*, vol. 35, pt. 1-2 (1960), p. 31-61.

This study makes the point that, although the Bedouin exist as a social force in Saudi Arabia, they are considerably outnumbered by the settled population and probably always have been 'if one distinguishes between real nomads and various gradations of partial nomads. In addition, Bedouin life is being profoundly affected by changes which include the establishment of order and unity and of a firm economic basis of life, higher living standards, and the end of Arabia's relative isolation. The bulk of the article is concerned with a survey of the geography of Arabia, and the various tribes, and the place of the Bedouin in the contemporary Arabian scene. The article concludes with a supplement giving a brief statistical estimate of Arabian Bedouin and semi-Bedouin tribes.

Population and Social Structure

422 The demography of the Middle East.
Georges Sabach. *Middle East Studies Association Bulletin,* vol. 4, pt. 2 (1970), p. 1-19.

Although it does not deal specifically with Saudi Arabia this article is included because it considers the various sources of demographic data available, the pressing need for accurate data, and specific information which needs to be collected. In addition to the sources of population data, the author also considers growth in demographic training and research, and major topics of demographic studies of the Middle East, especially in the vital areas of fertility and migration.

423 Fertility patterns and their determinants in the Arab Middle East.
T. Paul Schultz, Julie Da Vanzo. Santa Monica, California: Rand Corporation, 1970. 116p. (Research Memorandum RM 5978-FF).

This covers a wider area than Saudi Arabia. It examines the dimensions of population growth, particularly in the urban situation, and examines the social determinants of high fertility. The evidence is then seen in relation to the policy decisions that need to be taken by the respective governments.

424 The Badu of south-west Arabia.
Wilfred P. Thesiger. *Journal of the Royal Central Asian Society,* vol. 37, pt. 1 (1950), p. 53-61.

The text of a lecture given to the Society in 1949, dealing with the Bedouin who live in the empty quarter. Thesiger deals with their social life, the laws of hospitality, their love of poetry, and the constant struggle for survival in an unrelenting environment.

Saudi Arabia today: introduction to the richest oil power.
See item no. 10.

The Middle East: a handbook.
See item no. 24.

The Near East: a modern history.
See item no. 73.

The Middle East: a geographical study.
See item no. 142.

Saudi Arabia 2000: a strategy for growth.
See item no. 496.

Riyadh and the central province.
See item no. 518.

The economies of the Arab world: development since 1945.
See item no. 526.

Housing in Saudi Arabia and the Arab countries of the Gulf.
See item no. 673.

Social Change

425 **The changing world of the nomads.**
A. M. Abou-Zeid. In: *Contributions to Mediterranean sociology: Mediterranean rural communities and social change.* Edited by Jean G. Peristiany. The Hague: Mouton; New York: Humanities Press, 1968.

426 **The nomad problem and the implementation of a nomadic settlement scheme in Saudi Arabia.**
Hani Abdul-Hameed Akkad. In: *Land policy in the Near East.* Edited by M. R. el-Ghanemy. Rome: Food and Agricultural Organization, 1967, p. 296-308.

A significant contribution by the head of the Haradh Settlement Project in the Ministry of Agriculture. He begins by outlining the general background in Saudi Arabia, and the nomadic and semi-nomadic population which evolved because of economics. 'This economic phenomenon has created out of necessity the nomadic social structure, which is the most efficient for existence under the natural conditions prevalent in the desert.' He then considers the economic and social problems caused by nomadism, especially the effects of the lengthy drought cycle, and the methods of dealing with this, beginning with hydrological and soil surveys, and temporary measures to alleviate the immediate difficulties. The latter part of the article deals with the Haradh Project, which is located 270 kilometers south-southwest of Riyadh. The initial planning for the project began in 1964 and, although various sections of the report were not finalized, funds were allocated for a five-year period beginning 1965/66. The irrigation system, and the drainage system which is essential because of the salinity of the water, are described. The author then deals with the agricultural aspects, including training, housing and services, communications and costs of implementation.

Social Change

427 At the drop of a veil.
Marianne Alireza. Boston, Massachusetts: Houghton, Mifflin, 1971; London: Hale, 1972. 240p.

A very readable account of gradual moves towards female emancipation in the Arabian peninsula, written from the feminine viewpoint. A better book than Linda Blandford's *Oil sheikhs* (q.v.), although now superseded by events.

428 Man in arid lands. I: Endemic cultures. II: Patterns of occupance.
D. H. K. Amiran. In: *Arid lands: a geographical appraisal.* Edited by E. Sherbon Hills. London: Methuen; New York: Barnes & Noble, 1966, p. 219-54.

429 Nomadism in the Arab lands of the Middle East.
H. Awad. *Arid Zone Research*, vol. 18 (1962), p. 325-39.

Paper presented at the Problems of the Arid Zone Symposium held under the auspices of UNESCO at Paris in 1960.

430 Settlement of nomadic and semi-nomadic tribal groups.
Mohamed Awad. *International Labour Review*, vol. 79, pt. 1 (1959), p. 27-60. maps.

This is in two parts; the bulk of the article is concerned with the question in general, and this is followed by a short country by country survey, with rather cursory treatment of Saudi Arabia on p. 51-4. The first topic considered is the living conditions of the various tribal groups and the nomadic way of life. This leads to the subject of the encouragement of settlement either by direct or indirect methods, and the problems following settlement. Tribal groupings form more than half of the population of Saudi Arabia: 'It seems desirable that the economic integration of the tribes through sedentarization should be followed by their social integration....It should never be forced but should be left to the more gradual evolution of society and social institutions...'.

431 Bedouin, giving up the wild life.
Guardian, (4 Sept. 1970), p. 4.

An article on the resettlement programme.

432 Oil sheikhs.
Linda Blandford. London: Weidenfeld & Nicolson, 1976. 286p.

The dust jacket of this book describes it as remarkable in that a woman journalist 'penetrated the barriers [of Arab society] and tells the real story in personal and human terms of life in the walled gardens of present-day Arab society'. The section on Saudi Arabia appears on p. 43-144.

433 Sexual apartheid in Saudi Arabia.

Alan Butler. *New Society*, (6 July 1978), p. 13-15.

Discusses the position of women in society, which has not changed in Saudi Arabia, despite the other social and economic developments that have taken place.

434 Nomads of the nomads: the al Murrah Bedouin of the empty quarter.

Donald Powell Cole. Northbrook, Illinois: AHM Publishing Corporation, 1975. 179p.

The al Murrah tribe, numbering some 15,000 persons, occupies an area in the southeast of Saudi Arabia which includes the Rub' al Khali. The author, who lived amongst the tribe for eighteen months, discusses the social organization of Bedouin households, the social divisions within the tribe, and the role played by Islam. Also examined are the failed resettlement project at Haradh and the moves towards settlement among the al Murrah, with reference to the views of the Bedouin themselves. The author argues that the best hope for the survival of the al Murrah culture and social organization is for them to adapt to market-oriented pastoralism, so that they will continue to utilize the seasonal pastures of the desert.

435 The end of Arabia's isolation.

Gerald De Gaury. *Foreign Affairs*, vol. 25 (1946), p. 82-9. map.

An examination of the effects of oil exploration on Saudi Arabia's relations with other countries, and the effects that this change was likely to have upon traditional society. The author concludes, however, that despite problems the strength of Islam 'should enable them to face the future more confidently than would at first seem likely from the sharpness of the readjustment which faces them'.

436 A basis of operation for the nomads of the desert: development aspects of settling nomads in Saudi Arabia and Ethiopia.

H. Deguin. *Orient* (Germany), vol. 14 (1975), p. 177-8.

This article looks at the resettling of the nomads at al Haradh, a programme for which the planners had to have factual information about population numbers and density, consumption behaviour and literacy percentages. Because of the nature of the nomadic way of life, new methods of assessment had to be used, and planning and implementation took six years. The author argues for more flexibility in planning nomadic settlement and emphasizes the need to couple, with agricultural and economic development, strong social features.

437 A biographical approach to the study of social change in the Middle East: Abdullah Tanka as a new man.

Stephen Duguid. *International Journal of Middle East Studies*, vol. 1, pt. 3 (1970), p. 195-220.

It has been recognized that social change is necessary in the Middle East, but differences remain concerning the type of change, and the speed with which it should be introduced. The differences are based on the conflicting approaches of the three main groups, the traditionalists, the generation in power between 1918 and 1945, and the new generation of western-trained technocrats and administrators. The author has chosen to explore the viewpoints of the new generation through the attitudes of

Social Change

Abdullah Tanka, a former minister of petroleum and mineral affairs in Saudi Arabia. The reasons for the choice are that he represents a new generation in a traditionalist country, and has had close connections with the oil industry both as a minister and a consultant, and as an exile in Beirut from 1962.

438 The future of the Bedouin of northern Arabia.

W. G. Elphinston. *International Affairs,* vol. 21 (1945), p. 370-5.

439 Model of rural housing for Saudi Arabia.

Hassan Fathy. *Ekistics,* vol. 22 (1966), p. 203-4.

The village of Baesis is used as an example in a study of resettlement housing. Modular elements are used but sufficient variety is retained to accommodate a typical cross-section of village population, and the best of traditional architecture, together with open plans and private open places. The article shows the plans of a block which separates vehicular and animal traffic, and supports forty-five two-storey houses of varying sizes. The two remaining plans are for the ground and upper floors of houses whose owners have domestic animals. The houses are grouped around a walkway, but have traffic routes on either side to allow the animals to have direct access to the houses. The walkways are roofed over to allow more space and to provide relief from the sun.

440 The impact of the technological era.

Peter Flinn. *Journal of Contemporary History,* vol. 3, pt 3 (1969), p. 53-68.

Although this article covers the Middle East as a whole, the theme is of particular importance to any consideration of Saudi Arabia, which has been exposed to the new technology especially in the fields of oil and air transport. The author also discusses the effects of mass communications as a means of disseminating new ideas to a populace with a high incidence of illiteracy. One of the problems to be faced is the effect that these changes will have on a traditional society, and the author makes the point that 'the new men must necessarily create places for themselves in society which are new to Saudi tradition'.

441 Bedouin settlement in Saudi Arabia.

Alan George. *Middle East International,* no. 51 (Sept. 1975), p. 27-30. map.

An examination of the moves toward settlement of the nomads of Saudi Arabia, who are thought to account for about 60 per cent of the population. This trend began at the beginning of the 20th century with the establishment of settlements for the Ikhwan, but the process has since been accelerated by the oil industry and the oil revenues. The author examines the effects of the oil industry on nomadism, not only from the aspect of employment for the Bedouin, but also with reference to the facilities created as a by-product of the industry in terms of roads, water wells, and a demand for services.

442 The politics of social change in the Middle East and North Africa.

Manfred Halpern. Princeton, New Jersey; London: Princeton University Press, 1963. 462p. (Rand Corporation Research Studies).

A consideration of the effects of social change on the traditional infrastructure in the area.

443 Ecological consequences of Bedouin settlement in Saudi Arabia.

H. F. Hardy. In: *The careless technology: ecology and international development.* Edited by M. Taghi Farvar and John P. Milton. New York: Natural History Press, 1972, p. 683-93.

Discusses the ecological implications of moves towards settlement of the Bedouin. The author makes the point that in general terms nomadism is seen as wasteful of the resources of the environment, and settlement is to be encouraged, but this transition also brings its own problems.

444 The Bedouins and tribal life in Saudi Arabia.

A. S. Helaissi. *International Social Science Journal*, vol. 11, pt. 4 (1959), p. 532-8.

In discussing the nomadic question in Saudi Arabia, the author examines first the rapid social developments which have taken place in Saudi Arabia, mainly as a result of the income from oil. Consideration is given to progress in education and communications, and advances in health services, and these aspects are examined with particular regard to the problems arising from the assimilation of the Bedouins into urban areas. Other important aspects are the effects of increased mechanization in agriculture, and the influence of artesian wells on Bedouin life. Finally, attention is given to the efforts of the government to help the development of the Bedouins, whom the author considers represent some 50-60 per cent of the population.

445 The desert Bedouin and his future.

C. S. Jarvis. *Journal of the Royal Central Asian Society*, vol. 23, pt. 4 (1963), p. 585-93.

Although not strictly concerned with Saudi Arabia, as the author deals mainly with Sinai and Transjordan, this article is included because the basic concepts are relevant to the nomadic problems in Saudi Arabia. The author argues that change should be on a small scale to begin with, in order that the Bedouin are not frightened off by all the trappings of civilization that a large-scale operation would bring. 'The only way to save the Bedouin from extinction is to slowly ween him from his present haphazard existence and gradually settle him on his own land,...but the task...is a most difficult and heart-breaking one'.

446 Bedouin village: a study of a Saudi Arabian people in transition.

Motoko Katakura. Tokyo: University of Tokyo Press, 1977. 189p. maps. bibliog.

This social science study is centred on the Wadi Fatima near Mecca and in particular the village of Bushur. The work is particularly strong on the position of women in society, an area much of which lies beyond the reach of a male researcher. One interesting fact which emerges is that in 1970 31 per cent of the community, age six and over, were literate.

447 A house built on sand: a political economy of Saudi Arabia.
Helen Lackner.   London: Ithaca Press, 1978. 224p. maps.

A critical analysis of Saudi Arabian society, which aims to provide a basis for a better understanding both of the internal situation, and of Saudi Arabia's external relationships. The book begins by briefly considering the history of Arabia up to the beginning of the 20th century and the formation of the kingdom of Saudi Arabia. This leads to an account of the discovery of oil and the country's move into the area of international politics. An important section is that dealing with the state and the position of the ruling family as a political force, the state structures, and political opposition. An examination of Saudi Arabia's foreign policy, and the economy and development plans, all of which are linked, is followed by a discussion of the transitional state of the country's society, and especially the role of women in society, and the problem of the large migrant population. The author feels that these changes are at present 'causing cultural destruction without offering a replacement. The culture of the desert gives way to a cultural desert'.

448 The Bedouin and 'progress'.
W. O. Lancaster.   *Middle East International*, no. 79 (Jan. 1978), p. 26-7.

Moves towards settlement of the Bedouin do not necessarily mean progress, as changes in the way of life can, the author argues, be detrimental not only to the environment but to the Bedouin themselves. He begins by discussing the basis of the traditional Bedouin economy, and the reasons for the changes which were evident before they became government policy. The initial factors were the decline of the camel as an economically viable market animal, and a series of droughts between 1958 and 1962 which seriously depleted the camel population. On the other hand settled agriculture raised problems with regard to water supply, and the economically attractive sheep farming has a disastrous effect on the environment. In conclusion the author argues the case for a reversion to a camel-based economy which exists in harmony with the environment. 'And if it doesn't work? Well, at least no harm is done. The desert may not turn into a golden cornfield, but at least it won't become a barren waste'.

449 Bedouin in the oil economy.
W. O. Lancaster.   *Middle East International*, no. 74 (Aug. 1977), p. 26-7.

Changes in the Bedouin way of life were caused by the advent of oil and industrialization, and this will have serious implications for the future. However, this article examines the greater impact of the suppression of raiding, once the mainstay of the Bedouin economy, and the drought disaster from 1958 to 1962.

450 The evolution of Muslim urban society.
I. M. Lapidus.   *Contemporary Studies in Social History*, vol. 15 (1973), p. 21-50.

Discusses the gradual evolution toward an urban society.

451 Tradition and reform in Saudi Arabia.

George Lenczowski. *Current History*, no. 306, vol. 52 (Feb. 1967), p. 98-104.

Deals with the conflict between the traditional and progressive forces operating in Saudi Arabia, though it is stressed that King Faisal's approach was one of gradual evolution. The conflict is also seen in the wider context of the Arab world, and the author feels that the policies of Nasser and his allies represented an unacceptable outlook for a meaningful relationship between this bloc and King Faisal.

452 Sixty years of Arab social evolution.

Stephen H. Longrigg. *Asian Affairs*, vol. 60, pt. 1 (1973), p. 17-26.

This is a general survey of the social evolution of the Arabian peninsula and, although geographically some sections are not relevant, the main thread of discussion is of value for a study of Saudi Arabia. The author illustrates and discusses the changes that have taken place since 1912, ending with the influences of the income from oil. 'How much human good and how much bad - how much gain or loss - has there been, or is there, in all this alleged progress?...I have my ready answer. It is that I simply don't know'.

453 The modernization of Saudi Arabia.

Muhammad J. Nadir. Washington, D.C.: Embassy of the kingdom of Saudi Arabia, 1971.

The author, at time of publication, was minister plenipotentiary at the Embassy, and therefore this presents an official Saudi Arabian view of the changes that have taken place.

454 From nomad society to new nation: Saudi Arabia.

Richard H. Nolte. In: *Expectant peoples: nationalism and development*. Edited by Kalman H. Silvert. New York: Random House, 1963, p. 77-94.

This contribution briefly considers the transition of Saudi Arabia from a nomadic society to a nation with an infrastructure, a booming economy, and a role in the world economy because of oil.

455 Golden river to golden road: society, culture and technical change in the Middle East.

Raphael Patai. Philadelphia, Pennsylvania: University of Pennsylvania Press, 1969. 3rd ed. 461p.

456 Nomadism on the Arabian peninsula: a general appraisal.

P. G. N. Peppelenbasch. *Tijdschrift voor Economische en Sociale Geografie*, vol. 49, pt. 6 (1968), p. 333-46. maps.

Although concerned with the whole peninsula, the bulk of this article deals with Saudi Arabia, mainly with regard to changes in the organization of nomadic society, caused by its decline, and the relationship between man and his environment. The author begins by discussing the accepted image of the nomad, which is mainly based on the reports of the early explorers, and follows this by a consideration of nomadism as a phenomenon, defining five requirements necessary for true nomadism. The real extent of nomadism is difficult to gauge because of widely varying assessments of numbers, due to a lack of occurate census figures, but it is thought that the nomadic population of Saudi Arabia is about 25 per cent of the total (see the items by George and Helaissi in this section for very different estimates). Nomadic life is at a crisis stage because the traditional way of life is changing owing to a decreasing demand for camels, the ending of raiding or protection as a source of revenue, and the disappearance of the caravans. In addition there is the government policy of sedentarization, and all these factors amount to 'a significant and indicative phenomenon of the early phases of the struggle as a non-industrialized society attempts to emerge from its present low level of development'.

457 The Middle East: analyzing social changes.
W. R. Polk. *Bulletin of the Atomic Scientists*, vol. 23 (1967), p. 12-19.

458 Emergence of a new middle class in Saudi Arabia.
William Rugh. *Middle East Journal*, vol. 27, pt. 1 (1973), p. 7-20.

The middle class in Saudi Arabia began to grow in the 1940s and was the product of modernization; its significance is seen as lying in the fact that its members 'are distinguished from the rest of the middle class by their reliance on secular, non-traditional knowledge to attain their positions'. The new middle class are the first group in Saudi Arabia that belong to a class not automatically, because of family ties, but because of personal qualifications.

459 The habitability of the Arabian desert.
Eldon Rutter. *Geographical Journal*, vol. 76 (1930), p. 512-15.

An account of the way of life of the Bedouin in relation to the topography of the Arabian desert.

460 Saudi Arabia today.
Texaco Star Bulletin, vol. 35, pt. 1 (1968), p. 2-10.

Describes a number of important projects for industrial and social development which were under way at the time of writing. The plans for settling the Bedouins of the al Murrah tribe at Wadi as-Sahba are examined with reference to the building of model villages for 1,000 families, the provision of an adequate water supply through the sinking of fifty-eight wells linked to an irrigation system, and the establishment of an experimental farm to train the Bedouins in modern farming methods. The article stresses the importance of the development of agriculture in Saudi Arabia, and discusses progress to date. Developments of the roads, port facilities and railways are described, and the effect of the introduction of television considered. The growth of provision for education is outlined with reference to the importance of this area of development, and the country's plans to diversify from reliance on oil are examined by citing examples of small and medium-sized manufacturing industries that have been established, such as the cement industry, which supplies the booming construction industry.

461 Spatial patterns of Bedouin settlement in Al-Qasim region, Saudi Arabia.

Ahmed A. Shamekh. Lexington, Kentucky: University of Kentucky, 1975. 315p.

A detailed description of one of the most interesting areas in central Nejd and its settlement patterns. The author discusses the process of sedentarization, which results from social and economic factors, and the resultant growth in urban development in the form of satellite suburbs to older towns.

462 Measuring the changing family consumption patterns of Aramco's Saudi Arab employees 1962 and 1968.

Thomas W. Shea. In: *The Arabian peninsula: society and politics*. Edited by Derek Hopwood. London: Allen & Unwin; Lotowa, New Jersey: Rowman & Littlefield, 1972. 320p.

Deals with a household expenditure survey carried out by the economics department of Aramco on a random sample of its employees, to produce a consumer price index which would illustrate how prices affect standards of living. Firstly the author examines the method adopted in selecting the sample, the designing of the questionnaire, the interview procedures and the terms used. The second part deals with the survey results, with reference to: (a) Size and composition of household; (b) Location of residence and commuter status of employees; (c) Home ownership status and physical characteristics of homes; (d) Levels of income and expenditure; (e) Household expenditure, per capita money expenditure, and per capita real expenditure; (f) Food expenditure; (g) Supplementary analyses and tables.

463 Saudi Arabia: expectant peoples, nationalism and development.

Edited by Kalman H. Silvert. New York: Random House, 1963. 489p.

Discusses the expectations of the Saudi Arabians, in the light of the strength brought about by the revenue from oil, and their political position in the Arabian peninsula.

464 Bedouin development in Saudi Arabia: the Haradh project.

R. Smithers. Beirut: Ford Foundation, 1966.

An examination of one of the major Bedouin resettlement programmes at an early stage in its development.

465 The changing Middle East: achievement and the road ahead.

Elias H. Tuma. *Middle East Journal*.

A study of the Arab countries and the process of change, though 'there is an apparent inconsistency between the rapid and comprehensive change and the realized effects. Reality seems to lag behind appearances so that the results are frequently exaggerated and disappointing'. The failure to attain objectives can be explained by the institutional anachronisms and peculiarities of the social structures of individual countries. In particular the author selects and deals with three major characteristics which need removal or modification. These are specified as structural disunity, cultural rigidity, and an unrealistic time perspective.

Social Change

466 **Development planning and social objectives in various countries in the Middle East.**
United Nations. New York: United Nations, 1967.

467 **Studies on development problems in selected countries in the Middle East.**
United Nations. New York: United Nations, 1973. 137p.

468 **Oil, social change and economic development in the Arabian peninsula.**
John J. Vianney. *Levante*, vol. 15, pt. 4 (1968), p. 45-8.
Surveys firstly the presence of oil and the oil companies in the Arabian peninsula, and then examines the question of social change and economic development. The most significant changes are judged to be in the fields of female education, adult education, and rural institutions.

469 **Traditional Arab communities in the modern world.**
W. Watt. *International Affairs*, vol. 44 (1968), p. 494-500.

The Middle East: a handbook.
See item no. 24.

The Near East: a modern history.
See item no. 73.

The Middle East: a geographical study.
See item no. 142.

The wells of Ibn Saud.
See item no. 216.

The United States and Saudi Arabia: a policy analysis.
See item no. 353.

Arabian jubilee.
See item no. 358.

The Bedouin.
See item no. 383.

Some social aspects of Bedouin settlements in Wadi Fatima, Saudi Arabia.
See item no. 418.

Bedouin life in contemporary Arabia.
See item no. 421.

Administrative reform in Saudi Arabia.
See item no. 482.

Recent economic and social developments in Saudi Arabia.
See item no. 505.

National science and technology policies in the Arab states: present situation and future outlook.
See item no. 517.

Requiem for the empty quarter.
See item no. 576.

Housing in Saudi Arabia and the Arab countries of the Gulf.
See item no. 673.

Jiddah: portrait of an Arabian city.
See item no. 674.

Aspects of Saudi Arabia through the ages.
See item no. 740.

Health and Medicine

470 **Building for the health care programme.**
Philip R. Groves.   *Royal Institute of British Architects Journal,*
vol. 83, pt. 6 (1976).

An account of the planning, design, and construction of eight hospitals and a health training institute, with the express aim of keeping in character with the traditional indigenous architecture of the region.

471 **Hospitals, Saudi Arabia.**
Architectural Review, (Jan. 1976), p. 159.

A description of hospital building projects.

472 **King Faisal Specialist Hospital.**
Royal Institute of British Architects Journal, vol. 83, pt. 6
(1976), p. 242-4.

An account of the design and construction of the King Faisal Hospital, which has 240 beds, specialist medical services and other facilities, including villas, flats, swimming pools, and a power house.

473 **The state of nutrition in the Arab Middle East.**
Vinayak N. Patwardhan, William J. Darby.   Nashville,
Tennessee: Vanderbilt University Press, 1972. 308p.

474 **Preventive medicine takes high priority.**
The Times (London), (23 Sept. 1976), p. IV.

A special report discussing the moves towards provision of a health service for Saudi Arabia and, in particular, preventive medicine among children and the Bedouin.

475 **The King Faisal medical city.**
Pearce Wright. *The Times* (London), (13 May 1975), p. I-X.

A special report on the King Faisal medical city which has been built in Riyadh at a cost, for the first stage, of £100 million. The author considers the various aspects including the computer services, the self-contained energy supplies, and the ancillary services which will house and serve the projected staff of 1200.

Some social aspects of Bedouin settlements in Wadi Fatima, Saudi Arabia.
See item no. 418.

Saudi Arabia: investment opportunities.
See item no. 521.

The economies of the Arab world: development since 1945.
See item no. 526.

Law and Constitution

476 Recent judicial developments in Saudi Arabia.
Muhammad Ibrahim Ahmad 'Ali, 'Abdul Wahab Abu
Sulaiman. *Journal of Islamic Corporative Law*, pt. 3 (1969),
p. 11-20.

Saudi Arabia, it is argued, is the only country which professes and practises Islamic law in its entirety. 'The continuous application of this law in this part of the world proves the competence of Islamic law in the face of any problem.' The main reason for this is that the adoption of the Hanbali school of law has left 'the door of al-'ijtihad [i.e., personal judgements] still open, enabling the judges and the government to adopt any solution or legal opinion which does not run counter to the main Islamic principles'. The important impact that this has on judicial and administrative matters is examined through the study of specific cases.

477 Constitutions, electoral laws, treaties of states in the Near and Middle East.
Compiled by Helen Clarkson Davis. Durham, North Carolina: Duke University Press, 1953. 2nd ed. 541p. Reprinted, New York: AMS Press, 1970.

A valuable guide: the first compilation on the subject in English. Some of the items included are translated into English for the first time.

478 The influence of Islamic law on contemporary Middle Eastern legal systems: the formation and binding force of contracts.
P. Nicholas Koundes. *Columbia Journal of Transnational Law*, vol. 9, pt. 2 (Fall 1970), p. 384-435.

An important article providing an understanding of the place occupied by Islamic Law in the Middle East, especially in relation to contracts. The first part of the article deals with the introduction and evolution of the system. The second part considers the operation of the law in the various countries of the area; the section on Saudi Arabia begins on p. 428. The Hanbali school is the official law of Saudi Arabia, and adherence to Islamic law is laid down by Article 6 of the Saudi Arabian constitution; it is therefore relevant to any contractual agreements concluded in the kingdom.

479 **The board of grievances in Saudi Arabia.**
David E. Long. *Middle East Journal*, vol. 27, pt. 1 (1973), p. 71-6.

An account of the structure and function of the Duvan al-Muzalim, which was established in 1955 as the highest administrative tribunal.

480 **Islamic law in contemporary states.**
Joseph Schacht. *American Journal of Comparative Law*, vol. 8, pt. 2 (1959), p. 133-47.

Discusses the application of Islamic law in various states, including Saudi Arabia.

481 **Saudi Arabia's judicial system.**
S. Solaim. *Middle East Journal*, vol. 25, pt. 3 (1971), p. 403-7.

Saudi Arabia.
See item no. 15.

The Middle East: a handbook.
See item no. 24.

The anatomy of the Saudi revolution.
See item no. 222.

Jiddah and the western province.
See item no. 511.

Administration

482 Administrative reform in Saudi Arabia.
Richard A. Chapman. *Journal of Administration Overseas,* vol. 13, pt. 2 (1974), p. 332-47.

The author considers that Saudi Arabia 'is now at a crucial stage of administrative reform and development, and little has been published in English-language academic journals about its administrative problems and progress'. In addition the country has exceptional problems, and an approach to reform and development all of its own. The first part of this article deals with the political system in Saudi Arabia, which is based on a monarchical system gradually moving towards ministerial rule, but with religion dictating the whole conduct of life and providing the intellectual framework within which other activity takes place. The history of Saudi Arabia is outlined, together with the development of the administrative framework, which is based on a form of Islamic democracy and a more formal regionalism which was introduced in 1963. The economy is examined with reference to the need for industrial diversification, the development of agriculture and water resources, and the nomadic settlement projects; it is stressed that changes create new challenges in terms of administration, as skilful management is needed to persuade people to alter their traditional attitudes. Social change is seen in relation to the shortage of manpower, especially trained manpower. This shortage will tend to hasten the emancipation and education of women, and professionally qualified Saudis will increasingly appreciate their importance and their potential power for influencing the pace of change, perhaps in the political system as well as in public administration. Changes in education are seen to be of prime importance, and the educational programme is examined with reference to such factors as the age of the population, and the crucial administrative need to relate educational requirements to jobs.

483 The Saudi Arabian Council of Ministers.
C. Harrington. *Middle East Journal,* vol. 12, pt. 1 (1958), p. 1-19.

The Council of Ministers is the most potent of all the organized bodies of the government because it derives its power directly from the king, although it was only established in its present form in 1953. The author examines the composition and role of the Council of Deputies, the establishment of the Council of Ministers, and its constitution and activities. He concludes by presenting a hypothetical example of how it functions and describes the various adjuncts to the Council such as the grievance board.

484 The Middle East: its governments and politics.

Abid A. al-Marayati (and others).   Belmont, California:
Duxbury Press, 1972. 516p. maps.

The section on Saudi Arabia is interdisciplinary, as the political situation cannot be considered in isolation from its history, culture, social structure or economic conditions. The background picture is followed by an analysis of the structure of the government and its policies, particularly since the Second World War.

485 Saudi Arabia: the new statute of the Council of Ministers.

H. St. John B. Philby.   *Middle East Journal,* vol. 12, pt. 3
(1958), p. 318-23.

The statute aimed at the restoration of Saudi Arabia's financial stability, and was limited to matters of procedure and administrative reform.

486 Income tax in Saudi Arabia.

Nizar Rafei.   *Bulletin International Fiscal,* vol. 23, pt. 10
(1969), p. 482-7.

A description of the tax structure applied at the time of writing in Saudi Arabia, a system designed to assist foreign individuals and companies with business interests in the country. The author describes the three kinds of income tax levied, the first being the *zakat* which is levied only on Saudi nationals and companies, and is due on all income and capital that has been retained for one year or more. The second tax is an additional one levied on petroleum- and hydrocarbon-producing companies, while the third is levied on the incomes of foreign individuals and firms, and this is analysed in detail.

487 Saudi Arabia: survival of traditional élites.

Manfred W. Wenner.   In: *Political élites and political
development in the Middle East.* By Frank Tachau. Cambridge,
Massachusetts; London: Schenkman, 1975, p. 157-90.

A discussion of the place of the ruling class in Saudi Arabia, which traces its role through the historical and economic development of Saudi Arabia. Consideration is given to the effects that changing economic fortunes have had on society and class structure, and therefore on the position of the traditional élites.

Saudi Arabia today: introduction to the richest oil power.
See item no. 10.

Saudi Arabia.
See item no. 15.

The Middle East: a handbook.
See item no. 24.

A pilgrim in Arabia.
See item no. 361.

National security challenge to Saudi Arabia.
See item no. 374.

A house built on sand: a political economy of Saudi Arabia.
See item no. 447.

Administration

Arab banking.
See item no. 490.

Economic report: Saudi Arabia.
See item no. 500.

National science and technology policies in the Arab states: present situation and future outlook.
See item no. 517.

Saudi Arabia: investment opportunities.
See item no. 521.

The economies of the Arab world: development since 1945.
See item no. 526.

Hasa: an Arabian oasis.
See item no. 653.

Co-operative development in the kingdom of Saudi Arabia.
See item no. 659.

The Economy

488 Arab economic growth and imbalances, 1945-70.
Galal A. Amin. *L'Egypte Contemporaine*, no. 350, vol. 63 (1972), p. 257-95.

A general economic survey of the Arab world during the period in question. Saudi Arabia figures largely in the latter part of the survey.

489 Ideology and economic growth in the Middle East.
Johanger Amuzegor. *Middle East Journal*, vol. 28, pt. 1 (1974), p. 1-9.

A general discussion of the effects of political ideology on economic growth in the Middle East. Saudi Arabia is dealt with as part of this general study, classified in the 'non-socialist' camp and classed as an economy based on 'people's capitalism', with a large public sector, due to the oil-based nature of the economy.

490 Arab banking.
Guardian, (5 June 1978), p. 11-16. map.

A *Guardian* special report presenting a general survey of banking in the Middle East. The Saudi Arabian coverage explains and stresses the role of the Saudi Arabian Monetary Agency in the control of that particular sector of the economy.

491 Banking in the Arab world.
Arab Economist, no. 55, vol. 5 (Aug. 1973), complete issue.

The issue is divided into two sections, the first being a study by topic, and the second a survey by country. The general section presents viewpoints on banking conditions in the Arab world based on the results of a questionnaire, a comparative study of banking laws and regulations, and selected documentation on banking in the Arab world. Saudi Arabia is dealt with on p. 68-70.

The Economy

492 State and economics in the Middle East: a society in transition.
Alfred Bonne.   New York: Greenwood Press, 1973. 2nd ed. 452p.

493 The second Saudi Arabian development plan.
H. Bowen-Jones.   *Middle East Yearbook*, (1977), p. 76-80.

In 1975 the Saudi Arabian development plan appeared, covering the period 1975-1980. The government was able to stress that it could be fully funded, while still allowing sufficient reserves to meet unexpected contingencies. The author discusses the development plan against the background of Saudi Arabia being 'the only major oil producer in which the growth of proven reserves remains higher than the growth in extraction rates', and he notes that 'Saudi Arabia is assured of a vast income for perhaps a century at least, and is the only oil producer likely to be in financial surplus in the mid 1980s'.

494 A structural econometric model of the Saudi Arabian economy, 1960-70.
Faisal Safoog al-Bushir.   New York: Wiley, 1977. 134pp.

Detailed examination of the Saudi Arabian economy, using a model to test the progress of its development.

495 The economic challenge of the Arabs.
Gian Paolo Casadio.   Lexington, Massachusetts: Lexington Books, 1976; London: Saxon House, 1977. 232p.

A comprehensive examination of the problems faced by the Arab states, including Saudi Arabia, in the wake of the 1973 oil price rises. The author has produced a valuable work which examines the problems of using the oil wealth wisely, to ensure continued stability for the time when the oil runs dry. This economic problem is also seen in relation to the question of social change and political stability. Also examined are the financial structure of the producing states, and the potential in agriculture, manufacturing, and natural resources other than oil. Consideration is given to the links between the producer and the consumer, and the need for multilateral co-operation to ensure controlled industrial development.

496 Saudi Arabia 2000: a strategy for growth.
Jean Paul Cleron.   London: Croom Helm, 1978. 168p. bibliog.

A detailed examination of the Saudi Arabian economy, using a dynamic simulation model, which is experimented upon, and the results then commented on and analysed. The author also deals with the production of crude oil, the non-oil production, capital accumulation, domestic inflation, the Saudi population and labour force, and the relationship of Saudi Arabia with the rest of the world.

497 Economic development and population growth in the Middle East.

Charles A. Cooper, Sidney S. Alexander. London, New York: Elsevier, 1972. 620p.

A collection of studies dealing with the area as a whole, including Israel. The most relevant section is 'Prospects and problems of economic development of Saudi Arabia, Kuwait and the Gulf principalities', which presents useful data, but suffers from a lack of analysis.

498 Economic geography of Islamic countries.

Joseph de Samogyi. *Islamic Culture*, vol. 44, pt. 4 (1970), p. 197-226.

The introductory section deals with the geographical area of Islam, statistics of Islam, and the economic structural transformation in Islam. Specific mention, p. 214-16, of Saudi Arabia is mainly restricted to the economic aspects of oil.

499 Planning a region.

George Duncan. *Royal Institute of British Architects Journal*, vol. 83, pt. 6 (1976), p. 234-7.

An account of the work of the firm of Robert Matthew, Johnson-Marshall & Partners, who were retained by the Saudi Ministry of the Interior's Department of Municipal Affairs to undertake a comprehensive programme of planning at regional, city and local level. The area covered by the company was the western region, which included the sensitive areas of Mecca and Medina and therefore needed close liaison with Saudi architects and planners, owing to the restricted access to the areas. The article is useful for the insight it gives into the problems arising from the nature of the country, and the limitations involved when operating in Saudi Arabia.

500 Economic report: Saudi Arabia.

Arab Economist, no. 60 (Jan. 1974), p. 58-61.

A general report on the economy of Saudi Arabia dealing with the various sectors of the economy, including the pilgrimage.

501 Planning for economic development in Saudi Arabia.

David G. Edens, William P. Snavely. *Middle East Journal*, vol. 24, pt. 1 (1970), p. 17-30.

The authors selected Saudi Arabia as a subject for discussion because it is 'an example of an Arab nation which has begun to employ deliberate public policies and plans to increase economic welfare in an essentially free enterprise environment'. The article discusses the prospects for economic development under the following headings: 1. The meaning of planning and its prerequisites; 2. Environmental factors in the economic development of Saudi Arabia; 3. The development of formal planning in Saudi Arabia; 4. Resource allocation according to royal goals.

502 Problems of economic growth in oil producing countries: a case study in Saudi Arabia.

Hani S. Emam. *Arab Journal*, vol. 2, pt. 1 (1965), p. 16-24.

The choice of Saudi Arabia for a case study was made because of the economic consequences of a heavy inflow of capital into an underpopulated society. The author summarizes the major problems to be faced, the *laissez-faire* economic policy, the economic problems of 1956-59, and the problems of savings and capital formation. In planning development 'emphasis should be put on the expansion of domestic agricultural production. Foods and fibres, if produced domestically in sufficient quantities, would release large sums of foreign exchange now used for their import....Foreign exchange shortages may become still more serious when the country's industrial development gets under way and the demand for imported capital equipment grows'.

503 Local entrepreneurship in Saudi Arabia.

Richard N. Farmer. *Business History Review*, vol. 33, pt. 1 (1959), p. 73-86.

A study of the problems of carrying on a 20th century business in an economy still rooted in the 15th century. The author examines the career of one Saudi Arabian who progressed from labouring for Aramco to the ownership of a large contracting company. The influence on the development of local business by Aramco has been significant, in that the company's investments have pushed development ahead by hundreds of years. Such swift progress meant that local businessmen had to learn a new set of business rules in order to compete with and to supply companies based on Western business methods.

504 A hundred million dollars a day: inside the world of Middle East money.

Michael Field. London: Sidgwick & Jackson, 1975; New York: Praeger, 1976. 240p.

The author begins by discussing the arrival of OPEC and its effect, especially on the distribution of revenue within the Arabian peninsula. The book also discusses the question of government surplus funds, and the problems of recycling, in the context of international economics.

505 Recent economic and social developments in Saudi Arabia.

A. McKie Frood. *Geography*, vol. 24 (1939), p. 162-70. maps.

Surveys the economic and social changes which accompanied the political integration of Saudi Arabia. The author deals with the growth of internal communications, which has hastened the growth of political unity, and brought economic improvement as well. Oil and agriculture are also considered briefly, as are the effects of the new agricultural communities on the traditional tribal organization of the country.

506 Arab capital and international finance.

Abdlatif Y. al-Hamad. *Banker*, no. 575, vol. 124 (1974), p. 25-8.

A short examination by a director of the Kuwait Fund for Arab Economic Development of the growth of foreign exchange reserves and its effect on the stability of international financial markets.

507 Land of the Arabs.

M. Abdel-Kader Hatem. London: Longman, 1977. 323p. maps.

The theme of this work is the utilization of land and of water, tracing the history of agriculture, irrigation and land tenure. The Saudi Arabian section, p. 273-85, deals with the four regions: the Nejd, the Hedjaz, al-Hasa and 'Asir. Also considered are the agricultural experiments, Bedouin resettlement, the use of dams, and international co-operation.

508 Saudi Arabian Monetary Agency.

S. Hitti, G. Abed.   Washington, D.C.: United Nations, 1974 (Staff paper, XXI-2).

A briefing paper, outlining the history and functions of the agency, which is the main financial institution in the government of Saudi Arabia.

509 Jiddah: Saudi Arabia's west coast boom town.

H. Hopper.   *Lands East*, 1956, nos. 4-6, p. 11-17.

An examination of the position of Jeddah in the economy of Saudi Arabia, as the commercial centre of the western province and the main port for the pilgrimage.

510 Reconstruction and development projects in the kingdom of Saudi Arabia.

Rajai al-Husaini.   *Al Abhath*, (Sept. 1955), p. 343-62.

511 Jiddah and the western province.

The Times (London), (4 Nov. 1977), p. I-XVI. maps.

A special report on the key regions of Saudi Arabia, covering the boom in business, ports, banking, the city of Taif, fishing, transportation, commercial law, and the pilgrimage. These special reports of *The Times* are valuable as up-to-date surveys of particular topics.

512 Saudi Arabia's economy at the beginning of the 1970s.

Ramon Knauerhase.   *Middle East Journal*, vol. 28, pt. 2 (1974), p. 126-40.

This study concentrates on the period from 1962 to 1972 and aims to present a brief description of the Saudi Arabian economy, and to show the considerable progress that has been made. The kingdom is seen as having five economic regions tenuously linked by air, and by some surfaced roads. Consideration is given to the position of oil in the economy, and the significance of Petromin as an agent of industrial diversification. Whilst presenting a portrait of a booming economy, the author warns of a number of social and economic constraints which need to be removed if development is to proceed, especially with regard to replacement or rebuilding of plant, and the need to improve agriculture in order to create employment opportunities and to reduce imports.

513 Main outlines of the development plan of the kingdom of Saudi Arabia.

Economic Bulletin of the National Bank of Egypt, vol. 25, pt. 1-2 (1972), p. 45-60.

A summary of the 1970/71-1974/75 development plan. The plan aimed for the growth rate of the gross national product to be raised to 10 per cent per annum, for the development of human resources and, more importantly, for the diversification of the sources of national income.

The Economy

514 Mecca hotel and conference centre.
Royal Institute of British Architects Journal, vol. 83, pt. 6 (1976), p. 254-9.

The hotel and conference centre at Mecca was built as a result of an architectural competition, held initially for a complex at Riyadh but later extended to include one at Mecca. The article describes the hotel and conference centre, and considers the problems associated with operating in a restricted area of Saudi Arabia.

515 Middle East banking and finance.
Financial Times (London), (5 July 1977). 26p.

A special *Financial Times* survey of the Middle East banking and financial situation, especially in Saudi Arabia and Kuwait which have, and will have, the heaviest concentration of oil surplus. The conclusion is that although the region is using funds for development, and playing an active part in recycling funds, an Arab capital market has not yet been established.

516 Monetary problems of Saudi Arabia.
R. F. Mikesell. *Middle East Journal,* vol. 1, pt. 1 (1947), p. 169-79.

Discusses the financial problems experienced by Saudi Arabia, and the uncertainty of the economic structure.

517 National science and technology policies in the Arab states: present situation and future outlook.
Paris: Unesco, 1976. 214p.

The first section deals with the general features of the area, covering population, water resources, renewable natural resources, non-renewable natural resources, education, etc., providing a useful survey of the Arab world as a whole. Section 2 deals with national development plans in general terms, leading into section 3 which contains the country by country survey (Saudi Arabia p. 151-7). The last two sections deal generally with the building up of the national potential, and the objectives and constraints in the field of science and technology.

518 Riyadh and the central province.
The Times (London), (21 Oct. 1977), I-X.

The first of two special reports dealing with key regions of Saudi Arabia (see also special report on Jeddah, 'Jiddah and the western province', earlier in this section). The report deals with the construction boom, social life, agriculture, education, sport, and archaeology.

519 Banking regulations in Saudi Arabia.
J. O. Ronall. *Middle East Journal,* vol. 21, pt. 3 (1967), p. 399-402.

Discusses the evolution of the banking regulation system, the regulation of the 1952 law, and the provisions and significance of the 1966 law.

520 Saudi Arabia: development projects and allocations.
Arab Economist, no. 51, vol. 5 (April 1973), p. 66-70.

521 Saudi Arabia: investment opportunities.
Arab Economist, no. 51, vol. 5 (April 1973), p. 44-6.

A discussion of the financial allocations under the Development Plan (1970-1975), examining the various sectors of allocation, and the particular growth objectives compared to those realized in 1965/66.

522 Saudi Arabia: some British work.
Royal Institute of British Architects Journal, vol. 83, pt. 6 (1976), p. 234-59.

In addition to articles separately described, this issue has articles and reports too brief to merit individual description. The following reports fall into this category: Government Centre, Taif, p. 238; Palace interiors, Riyadh, p. 249; Taif City Hall, p. 249; Colour television complex, Abha, p. 250; Staff housing, Dubai and Quarayat, p. 250; Mosque in Riyadh, p. 251-3.

523 Saudi Arabia - special supplement.
Arab Economist, no. 65, vol. 6 (June 1974), p. 4-70 (and statistical appendix).

A special supplement presenting a valuable survey of the Saudi Arabian economy, covering all aspects of development, and accompanied by a useful statistical appendix. The specialist articles are considered in the relevant sections under the individual contributors.

524 A Saudi white elephant?
New Internationalist, no. 61 (March 1978), p. 21-2.

An examination of the Saudi oil-based economy in which development is going on apace, mainly in small quick profit areas. In essence, the economy depends on expatriate labour at all levels, and no end is foreseen to the requirement as 'it seems that there will always have to be a large imported workforce to maintain the industries that never really benefit the Saudis themselves'.

525 The determinants of Arab economic development.
Yusif A. Sayigh. London: Croom Helm, 1978. 181p. bibliog.

An important and well-documented work which is the companion volume to the author's *The economies of the Arab world* (see next item). It is an in-depth exploration of the factors determining economic development in the Arab world. These factors are identified as economic, political, administrative, and socio-cultural, with additional sections devoted to the questions of petroleum and regional development. The concluding chapter deals with prospects for development in the countries surveyed in the companion volume, including Saudi Arabia.

526 The economies of the Arab world: development since 1945.
Yusif A. Sayigh. London: Croom Helm, 1978. 726p.

This book is a comprehensive and significant contribution to the literature of modern Arab economic development. The author introduces five main periods of development since 1945, and then proceeds to examine all aspects of the economy, supported by tables, statistics and references. A summary of the Saudi Arabian economy appears on p. 127-85.

527 Population growth, capital formation and economic growth in the Middle East.
Yusif A. Sayigh. *Proceedings of the World Population Congress, Belgrade,* (1965), vol. 4, p. 30-3.
A discussion of the role played by oil revenues in relation to increases in population and economic growth, and of the dangerous effect that economic growth can have on population increase.

528 Problems and prospects of development in the Arabian peninsula.
Yusif A. Sayigh. *International Journal of Middle East Studies,* vol. 2, pt. 1 (1971), p. 40-58.
This is an important study of development in the Arabian peninsula and, although discussion of Saudi Arabia forms only part of the paper, it is valuable for drawing comparisons with the other countries of the peninsula. The article is divided into two main sections which consider problems (p. 41-52), and prospects (p. 53-8), after a brief introduction. The text is supported by excellent statistical tables. Among the problem areas considered are those of education, acceptance of technological advance, health and sanitation, public administration, the narrowness of the economic base, and political fragmentation of the area. In the matter of prospects the author considers that any evaluation 'ought to be dynamic in nature and to take into account not only the 'natural' or obvious areas where there is prima facie a good case for resource development, but also those areas where changes in technology, the discovery of new resources, the development of manpower in terms of education and technical skills, and change in organization can lead to new resource combinations, the production of new products, and general improvement in economic performance'. This paper also appears in: *The Arabian peninsula: society and politics,* edited by Derek Hopwood, p. 286-303.

529 Long-term investment discouraged by stringent laws.
David Shirreff. *The Times* (London), (18 Feb. 1977), p. V.
A special report which discusses how the control of investment by the Saudi Arabian Monetary Agency is an obstacle to any long-term investment in the economy, and a deliberate attempt to avoid the banking and financial problems found elsewhere.

530 Saudi Arabia; with an account of the development of its natural resources.
Karl S. Twitchell (and others). Princeton, New Jersey: Princeton University Press, 1958. 3rd ed. 281p. maps.
A general survey of Saudi Arabia, with particular stress on its economic development and the impact of this development on the world economy. The section dealing with the development of natural resources is particularly valuable, because of Karl Twitchell's experience and activities in this field.

531 The aid programs of the OPEC countries.
M. Williams. *Foreign Affairs*, vol. 54, pt. 2 (1976), p. 308-24.

Concentrates mainly on Kuwait and Abu Dhabi, both of whom have long-established funds, but Saudi Arabia is also considered.

532 Financial reforms in Saudi Arabia.
A. N. Young. *Middle East Journal*, vol. 14, pt. 4 (1960), p. 466-9.

Deals with the measures taken during the period 1948-60 to stabilize the Saudi economy and financial institutions.

533 Saudi Arabian currency and finance.
Arthur N. Young. *Middle East Journal*, vol. 7 (1953), p. 361-80, 539-56.

534 New sources of funds and their effect on the international market.
Minas A. Zombanakis. New York: First Boston Corporation, 1974. 14p.

A paper presented by the managing director of First Boston (Europe) Ltd. discussing the possible effects of the oil surplus revenue on the international monetary market.

Saudi Arabia.
See item no. 7.

Saudi Arabia today: introduction to the richest oil power.
See item no. 10.

Saudi Arabia.
See item no. 15.

The Middle East: a handbook.
See item no. 24.

The Middle East: a geographical study.
See item no. 142.

Jiddah: portrait of an Arabian city.
See item no. 674.

Oil

General

535 The world petroleum market.
M. A. Adelman.   Baltimore, Maryland; London: Johns
Hopkins Press, 1974. New ed. 438p.
Published for *Resources for the Future Quarterly*.

536 Arab petroleum.
Central Bank of Egypt Economic Review, vol. 7, pt. 1-2 (1967),
p. 37-61.
A survey article in two parts, the first dealing with the petroleum industry in general:
the early explorations; production and reserves; and, income and investment. The
second part of the article is a very brief country by country survey.

537 B.P. statistical review of the world oil industry.
British Petroleum Ltd.   London: British Petroleum (annual).
Among topics considered are oil reserves, production, consumption, trade, refining,
shipping, and energy sources and consumption. Finally there is an historical section
covering the previous ten years. The information is in the form of statistical tables and
graphs.

538 An oil-full economy.
Y. T. el-Zein.   *Arab Economist*, no. 65, vol. 6 (1974), p.
9-17.
A consideration, in a special supplement on Saudi Arabia, of the country's oil
policies, which are seen as having widespread repercussions around the world in
addition to their effects on the Saudi economy. The author considers five major
objectives as the focal points of the Saudi oil policy: (a) A larger degree of direct
Saudi control over the oil sector; (b) Greater integration of the oil sector into the local
economy; (c) Oil distribution; (d) Utilization of oil revenue for economic develop-

ment; (e) Co-ordination of Saudi Arabian economic interests with world demand for oil.

539 Desert enterprise: the Middle East oil industry in its local environment.
David H. Finnie. Cambridge, Massachusetts; London: Harvard University Press, 1958. 224p.

540 Annual report.
General Petroleum and Mineral Organization. Riyadh: The Organization (annual).

Petromin is the body responsible for the promotion of petroleum and mineral industries, dealing with oil exploration, refining and marketing, petrochemicals, transportation and steel. As such the annual reports are of great importance to an understanding of economic developments in these fields. Also of importance is Petromin's education and training programme, through the Petromin University, and the various 'on the job' training programmes within its various operations.

541 Oil and public opinion in the Middle East.
David Hirst. London: Faber; New York: Praeger, 1966. 127p.

This book works on the premise that the oil industry is regarded with mistrust by the Arabs, and the author seeks to explain the nature and causes of this mistrust. The first part deals with the political, economic and legal aspects of Arab public opinion, while the second part uses Iraq and OPEC as case studies. The question of Saudi Arabia is considered as part of this study in general terms, and also specifically in relation to Aramco.

542 The economic history of the Middle East, 1800-1914.
Edited by Charles Philip Issawi. Chicago, Illinois; London: Chicago University Press, 1966. 543p.

A very useful work, especially for drawing comparisons between the present oil-based economies.

543 The economics of Middle Eastern oil.
Charles Philip Issawi, Mohammed Yeganeh. London: Faber, 1963. 230p.

Very good survey of the oil industries, and their significance in the economies of both the producing and the consuming states.

544 Oil, the Middle East and the world.
Charles Philip Issawi. London; Beverly Hills, California: Sage Publications, 1972. 86p. bibliog. (Washington Papers, no. 4).

An extremely useful work which deals with the following topics: 1. The energy patterns; 2. Middle Eastern oil: the economies; 3. Middle Eastern oil: the politics; 4. Prospects and politics.

545 **American culture in Saudi Arabia.**

Solon T. Kimball. *Transactions of the New York Academy of Sciences*, vol. 18 (1956), p. 469-84.

This article is really an account of the Aramco operation in the eastern province of Saudi Arabia, and the involvement of American personnel in its operations. In particular it deals with the facilities provided for the expatriate employees, the problems faced, and the way of life.

546 **The price of Middle East oil; an essay in political economy.**

W. A. Leeman. Ithaca, New York; London: Cornell University Press, 1962. 274p.

Explains the complex pricing structure for oil, and relates this to the political situation.

547 **Oil and state in the Middle East.**

George Lenczowski. Ithaca, New York; London: Cornell University Press, 1960. 379p. bibliog.

A very detailed examination, which considers the role of the producer, the influence of oil in the western economies, the concessions and legal safeguards, relations between oil companies and government, offshore legislation, border disputes, and the multinationals and nationalist tendencies. Also considered is the position of the employees vis-à-vis the host country, in terms of the impact that they make as a group on society, the interrelationship between workers of different countries, and the human aspects of operations such as wages, housing, and health services.

548 **Beyond the energy crisis.**

John Maddox. London: Hutchinson; New York: McGraw-Hill, 1975. 208p. bibliog.

An examination of the world energy situation in the light of the Middle East oil crisis of 1973. The book discusses the way in which this situation was reached, the effect of national control over the means of production, the role of OPEC, and the future energy requirements of the consuming nations.

549 **Problems of a common production policy among OPEC countries.**

Zuhair Mikdashi. *Middle East Economic Papers*, (1969), p. 53-68.

550 **Power play: the tumultuous world of Middle East oil, 1890-1973.**

Leonard Mosley. London: Weidenfeld & Nicolson; New York: Random House, 1973. 369p. maps.

This work deals with the development of the oil industry in the Middle East, through the granting of concessions, and the oil companies themselves. Also discussed are the political and economic changes which took place after the transfer of power from the oil companies to the producing countries. Consideration is also given to the use of oil as a political weapon, the effects of Libya on the oil market, and international political economics.

551 An economic geography of oil.
Peter R. O'Dell. London: Bell, 1963. 219p. maps. Reprinted, Westport, Connecticut: Greenwood Press, 1976.

A very useful work; the author is a noted and controversial commentator on the oil industry.

552 Oil production, revenues and economic development prospects for Iran...Saudi Arabia... Bahrain.
London: Economist Intelligence Unit, 1974. 59p. map. (Report no. 18).

Authoritative report of permanent reference value.

553 Statistical bulletin.
Organization of Petroleum Exporting Countries. Vienna: OPEC (annual).

A detailed statistical survey of the oil industry in the member countries. Invaluable as a source of statistical material.

554 OPEC and the petroleum industry.
Mana Sahed al-Otaiba. London: Croom Helm; New York: Halsted Press, 1975. 192p. bibliog.

A significant study by the U.A.E. minister of petroleum and mineral resources of the beginnings and evolution of OPEC, dealing not only with the structure of OPEC and its policies, but also with the oil industry in the member states. The organization is one of the most important developments in the history of the Middle East oil industry, not only from the economic but also from the political viewpoint.

555 The growth of firms, Middle East oil, and other essays.
Edith T. Penrose. London: Cass; Forest Grove, Oregon: International Scholarly Book Services, 1971. 336p.

A good introduction to the growth of the multinational oil companies.

556 The large international firm in developing countries: the international petroleum industry.
Edith T. Penrose. London: Allen & Unwin; Cambridge, Massachusetts: MIT Press, 1968. 311p. bibliog.

Discusses the role of the multinational oil companies in the oil-producing countries.

557 Oil and state in Arabia.
Edith T. Penrose. In: *The Arabian peninsula: society and politics.* Edited by D. Hopwood. London: Allen & Unwin; Lotowa, New Jersey: Rowman & Littlefield, 1972, p. 271ff.

An essay which discusses the relationship between oil and state in the Arabian peninsula; the governments' dominant role in the economy is reflected in the manner in which the oil revenue has been spent. The author gives a brief historical introduction, and discusses the concession system, and the role of the national oil companies.

Oil. General

558 The oil industry in the Middle East.
Edith T. Penrose. In: *The Middle East: a political and economic survey*. Edited by Peter Mansfield. London, New York: Oxford University Press, 1973. 4th ed., p. 111-23.

This thematic study deals with the region in general, including Saudi Arabia, and covers the discovery of oil, the concessions, moves towards profit-sharing, the establishment of OPEC, and the impact of oil on the Middle East by way of increased revenue, demands for labour, and moves towards modernization.

559 The role of Petromin and its future in Saudi Arabia.
World Petroleum, vol. 37 (1966), p. 12, 68.

Discusses the role of Petromin as the controlling organization for the entire oil-based and mineral-based activity in Saudi Arabia.

560 The seven sisters.
Anthony Sampson. London: Hodder & Stoughton; New York: Viking Press, 1975. 334p.

Although not solely concerned with the Arab world this book, which tells the story of the seven largest oil companies, deals with Saudi Arabia at some length, particularly with regard to her relations with Aramco. The author deals at length with the political implications in the producing states of the oil cartel, created by the companies, which was eventually countered by the creation of OPEC. In this connection the author concludes that 'OPEC owes its success in large measure to the internal divisions in the West...the transition was partly due to the West's inability to face up to a new situation until forced to'.

561 Review of the oil industry.
Saudi Arabia. Ministry of Petroleum and Mineral Resources. Dammam, Saudi Arabia: Ministry Technical Affairs Department, 1971. 127p.

This review gives information on oil exporting companies, concessions, geology, exploration, oil fields, production facilities and refining.

562 Oil and Arab regional development.
Kamal S. Sayegh. New York, London: Praeger, 1968. 357p. maps.

An assessment of the role of oil in possible future moves towards regional co-operation and development, in which Saudi Arabia would play a key role.

563 Oil: the biggest business.
Christopher Tugendhat, Adrian D. Hamilton. London: Eyre Methuen, 1975. Rev. ed. 404p. bibliog.

An important book which discusses the total development of the oil industry. The Middle East is dealt with in depth. The question of OPEC is also dealt with, and the problem of oil production versus preservation. In Saudi Arabia's case, the aim is to preserve reserves without endangering the economies of the developed world.

564 Saudi Arabian development strategy.
Donald A. Wells. Washington, D.C.: American Enterprise
Institute, 1976. 80p.

An examination of the Saudi Arabian development plans and their effect upon the
international money markets. These plans are also seen in relation to the pricing of oil,
the rate of production, and future political developments of relevance to Saudi Arabia
and her neighbours.

Saudi Arabia today: introduction to the richest oil power.
See item no. 10.

The Middle East: a handbook.
See item no. 24.

The Near East: a modern history.
See item no. 73.

The Middle East: a geographical study.
See item no. 142.

The wells of Ibn Saud.
See item no. 216.

The Persian Gulf in the twentieth century.
See item no. 346.

From nomad society to new nation: Saudi Arabia.
See item no. 454.

Saudi Arabia 2000: a strategy for growth.
See item no. 496.

**Saudi Arabia; with an account of the development of its natural
resources.**
See item no. 530.

Science and technology in the eastern Arab countries.
See item no. 661.

Petroleum statistical bulletin.
See item no. 718.

Oil exploration and development

565 All maps were blank: Arabia's great desert yields its secrets to oil explorers.
The Lamp, vol. 43, pt. 3 (1961), p. 16-21.

Oil. Oil exploration and development

566 **Geological conditions of oil occurrence in Middle East fields.**
N. E. Baker, F. R. S. Hanson. *Bulletin of the American Association of Petroleum Geology*, vol. 36, pt. 10 (1952), p. 1885-1901. maps.

This paper covers the Middle East in general, but seeks to gather together knowledge of known geological conditions, and to show the effect of these conditions on the generation and accumulation of oil.

567 **Saudi Arabia offshore field to go on production soon.**
H. T. Brundage. *World Oil*, vol. 144 (April 1957), p. 238-9, 256-61.

568 **Oil exploration in the Middle East.**
E. De Golyer. *Mines Magazine*, vol. 36, pt. 11 (1946), p. 491-6.

569 **Oil reserve provinces of Middle East and southern Soviet Russia.**
F. Julius Faths. *Bulletin of the American Association of Petroleum Geology*, vol. 31, pt. 8 (1947), p. 1372-83. maps.

A discussion of petroleum reserve areas, related mainly to a consideration of those controlled by Russia as compared to those controlled by the West, but the situation is now quite different because of the political changes that have taken place since the article was written.

570 **The oilfields of the Middle East.**
G. M. Lees. *Petroleum Times*, vol. 55 (27 July 1951), p. 651-4, 671.

A description of the oilfields of the Middle East, including Iran, dealing with the concessions, post-Second World War developments, the differing characteristics of the fields, and the areas to be explored. The statistical section of this article is only of historical significance.

571 **Oil in the Middle East: its discovery and development.**
Stephen Hemsley Longrigg. London, New York: Oxford University Press for the Royal Institute of International Affairs, 1968. 3rd ed. 519p. maps.

An extremely valuable work which is both authoritative and readable.

572 **Arabian oil ventures.**
H. St. John B. Philby. Washington, D.C.: Middle East Institute, 1964. 134p. maps.

An account of oil exploration in Saudi Arabia, leading to the 1933 negotiations which, in turn, led to the discovery of oil and its exploitation.

573 Saudi Arabia: looking for more oil.
Petroleum Economist, vol. 43, pt. 1 (1976), p. 14-16.
Reports of planned increases in production through development of existing fields and further exploration.

574 Stratigraphic relations of Arabian jurassic oil.
Max Steinke (and others). *Bulletin of the American Association of Petroleum Geology*, (June 1958), p. 1294-329.
Discusses the geological requirements for the creation of oil deposits.

575 Basic pattern of exploration in Saudi Arabia remains unchanged.
W. H. Thralls, R. C. Hassan. *Oil and Gas Journal*, vol. 55, pt. 28 (1957), p. 91-6.

576 Requiem for the empty quarter.
Michael Tomkinson. *Geographical Magazine*, vol. 43, pt. 3 (1970), p. 183-93. maps.
Deals mainly with oil exploration in the Rub' al-Khali but, at the same time, consideration is given to the nomadic population, wild life, water resources, and agricultural development on the edges of the empty quarter.

577 The miracle of Aramco.
James K. Westcott. *National and English Review*, vol. 137 (Dec. 1951), p. 344-9.

578 Saudi Arabian offshore legislation.
R. E. Young. *American Journal of International Law*, vol. 43, pt. 3 (1949), p. 530-2.
An outline of the legislation concerned with offshore exploration and exploitation of oil.

March arabesque.
See item no. 31.

Britain's moment in the Middle East, 1914-56.
See item no. 293.

Oil and state in the Middle East.
See item no. 547.

Concessions to national control

579 **Petroleum agreements in the Arab and other oil-producing countries.**
Mahmoud S. Amin. *L'Egypte Contemporaine*, no. 332, vol. 59 (1968), p. 23-42.

Considers the three main types of petroleum agreements, i.e. concessions, partnership agreements and contract agreements, and these types of agreements are related to the relevant countries and companies. The author also considers the modifications that have been made to the various agreements as the operations have developed. As many radical changes have taken place since this article was written its value is only historical, but it does provide a useful summary of the various agreements in force at that time.

580 **Aramco.**
Life, (28 March 1949), p. 62-79.

A general account of the operations of the Arabian American Oil Company, useful for its brief introduction to the early period of operations.

581 **Manpower and oil in Arab countries.**
Albert Y. Badre, Simon G. Siksek. Beirut: American University of Beirut. Economic Research Institute, 1959. 270p.

A general examination of labour problems in the oil industry, including Saudi Arabia, and of the management problems stemming from the difficulties which arise from the lack of a skilled indigenous work force.

582 **The evolution of oil concessions in the Middle East and North Africa.**
Henry Cattan. Dobbs Ferry, New York: Oceana, 1967. 173p. maps.

An invaluable account of the whole question of concessions in the area, including Saudi Arabia.

583 **Law of oil concessions in the Middle East and North Africa.**
Henry Cattan. Dobbs Ferry, New York: Oceana, 1976. 200p.

The standard work on the area: complex but important to an understanding of the oil industry.

584 **The new oil states.**
Jean-Marie Chevalier. London: Allen Lane, 1975. 187p. maps. bibliog.

This work deals with the changing situation in the oil industry brought about by the participation agreements concluded between the producing nations and the oil companies. It also places the importance of the oil industry in the context of the world economy, and deals with the international role of the oil companies.

585 Oil concessions in West Asia and the problem of revision.

K. H. Darja. *International Studies*, vol. 4, pt. 2 (Oct. 1962),
p. 143-68.

A discussion of the changing situation regarding the oil concessions, and the increasing influence of the producing nations who had become aware of their oil wealth. The author, while appreciating the need for revision of the original concessions, feels that 'legal protection of long term contractual relations between 'foreign private companies' and 'local governments' seems to require built-in procedures for fair and feasible revision, on demonstrably proper occasions'.

586 Middle East oil money and its future expenditure.

Nicholas Fallon. London: Graham & Trotman, 1975; New
York: International Publications Service, 1976. 240p. maps.
bibliog.

Begins by discussing the oil crisis of 1973-74 and its effect on oil prices and politics, and projecting these developments into the 1980s. The spending of revenues is discussed in relation to banking and financial institutions in the producing countries. The author discusses the major development and expenditure sectors, which began with a process of general development, though the main problem has been the shortage of human resources. Although this has been recognized in the educational programmes and progress has been made, there is still a shortage, particularly in the middle management areas. Various sectors such as natural gas, fertilizers, agriculture, communications and social developments are dealt with, followed by a country by country survey. Saudi Arabia is covered on p. 127-208.

587 Recruitment and training of labor: the Middle East oil industry.

David H. Finnie. *Middle East Journal*, vol. 12, pt. 2 (1958),
p. 127-43. map.

The author is concerned, as regards Saudi Arabia, with the operation of Aramco, which employs predominantly Saudi labour. At the time of writing, this presented problems in training as the majority of Saudis employed had little or no formal schooling; therefore, training ranged from primary education in the 'three Rs' to university courses.

588 Middle East oil in a revolutionary age.

George Lenczowski. Washington, D.C.: American Enterprise
Institute, 1976. 36p.

An examination of the evolution of the legal and economic position of the oil industry in relation to political and economic changes in the area. The author examines the motivation behind the use of oil as a political weapon and the position of Saudi Arabia as a restraining influence.

589 Coping with the Arab billions.

I. M. D. Little, Robert Mabro. *Financial Times* (London), (27
Dec. 1973), p. 21.

A consideration of the problems faced by the world economy in dealing with the absorption of the surplus funds of the Arab oil producers.

590 **Arab wealth from oil: problems of its investment.**
Robert Mabro, Elizabeth Monroe.   *International Affairs*, vol. 50 (Jan. 1974), p. 15-27.

An important article which looks at the problems faced by Arab countries in investing the income from oil. The authors trace the growth of the oil revenues and the reasons for the current revenue surplus. It details the present pattern of investment, and examines potential investment outlets which are felt not to be sufficient, in the Arab world alone, to absorb the surplus funds. The authors conclude by considering the possible impact on the world equity market of these surplus funds, the pitfalls in the future, and the policy implications both for the oil producers and the consumers.

591 **Participation policy of the producing countries in the international oil industry.**
S. Matsumara.   *Developing Economies*, vol. 10, pt. 1 (1972), p. 3-44.

Deals with the transfer of control from the oil companies to the producing governments.

592 **Spending oil revenues: development prospects in the Middle East to 1975.**
K. McLachlan.   London: Economist Intelligence Unit, 1972. (*Quarterly Economic Review* Special, no. 10).

Detailed look at the ways in which oil revenues are being spent in the producing states.

593 **Economic changes in Yemen, Aden and Dhofar.**
Alexander Melamid.   *Middle Eastern Affairs*, vol. 5, pt. 3 (1964), p. 88-91.

Discusses the influence of oil revenues from Saudi Arabia and her Gulf neighbours on the countries of southern Arabia who have no such financial base for economic growth.

594 **A financial analysis of Middle Eastern oil concessions, 1901-1965.**
Zuhayr Mikdashi.   New York, London: Praeger, 1966. 340p.

Examines the financial aspects of the Middle East oil concessions as they affected both the companies and the governments concerned.

595 **Foreign investment in the petroleum and mineral industries; case studies of investor-host country relations.**
Raymond F. Mikesell, William H. Bartosch (and others).   Baltimore, Maryland; London: Johns Hopkins Press, 1971. 459p.

The case study relevant to Saudi Arabia is by Donald A. Wells, and concerns Aramco as a challenge to private investment in the developing world.

596 Permanent sovereignty over oil resources: a study of Middle East oil concessions and legal change.

Muhammad Mughraby.   Beirut: Middle East Research and Publishing Center, 1966. 233p.

Examines the transfer of control over the means of production from concessions, through participation, to eventual national control.

597 A study of oil contract negotiations by Saudi Arabia with Aramco.

R. Narayanan.   *International Studies*, vol. 7, pt. 4 (1966), p. 568-81.

A discussion of the various contractual negotiations between Saudi Arabia and Aramco, which the author considers a unique case because it has not been subject to the problems met by oil companies elsewhere. The relationship is seen as a successful partnership because the elements of power in the relationship have inherent limitations. 'One of the partners, the Saudi Arabian government, represents the power of sovereignty. But the exercise of sovereign power is circumscribed, to a very great extent, by the government's dependence on Aramco, which is an important source of income. On the other hand, Aramco, which represents enormous economic power, is limited by the terms and obligations of the concession contracts granted by the Saudi Arabian government'. The author then proceeds to discuss the various contract negotiations: 1. Early oil contract negotiations; 2. The 'Gold Clause' controversy; 3. Fifty-fifty profit-sharing principle; 4. The Sidon claim; 5. The Onassis tanker dispute.

598 Petroleum politics, 1951-1974: a five-act drama reconstructed.

Dankwart A. Rustow.   *Dissent*, (Spring 1974), p. 144-53.

An account of the politics of oil presented as a drama in five acts: Act 1. Company control, 1951-1955. In this section consideration is given to the agreements between Aramco and Saudi Arabia, leading to the 50-50 profit-sharing agreement. Act 2. The stage expands, 1955-1970. Here the author examines the challenge by independent producers to the 'Seven Sisters', and the emergence on the scene of OPEC. Act 3. OPEC takes charge, 1970-1973. This deals with the increased tax being levied by OPEC, and changes in the status of the oil companies through nationalization, though in Saudi Arabia the agreement was for a scheme of participation, whereby the government was to take an immediate 25 per cent interest in the concessions, rising yearly to 51 per cent in 1981. Act. 4. The Arab 'oil weapon', 1973. An account of the Arab use of oil as an economic and political weapon during the Yom Kippur War, covering co-operation and lack of unity among the producers, the role of the oil companies, and the effect on the industrialized nations. After the political use of oil, the economic aspect emerged, with a 70 per cent increase in mid-October on the 'posted price', followed by a 128 per cent increase in December. Act 5. The $64 billion question. This deals with the new situation which resulted from the events of 1973, the effects on the consuming nations, the position of the Arab states in relation to conservation versus production, and the problem of dealing with the investment of surplus funds.

599 Saudi Arabia takeover in final stages.

Middle East, no. 18 (April 1976), p. 44.

A summary of the final stages of the takeover by Saudi Arabia of Aramco, including the producing fields, the refineries, and the liquified petroleum gas facilities.

600 **The legal framework for oil concessions in the Arab world.**
Simon G. Siksek. Beirut: Middle East Research and
Publishing Center, 1960. 140p. (Middle East Oil Monograph,
no. 2).

Important for an understanding of the basis on which the concessions were made, and
the conditions under which the oil companies operate.

601 **Oil: towards a new producer-consumer relationship.**
Sheikh Ahmed Zaki Yamani. *World Today* (Nov. 1974), p.
479-86.

This article is the text of a lecture, given at Chatham House, London, on 17
September 1974, and it begins with the statement that 'Saudi Arabia has always felt
the need for moderate and gradual price increases that cope with market conditions and
to which the consuming countries' economies can be adjusted'. The significance of the
lecture lies in the fact that the speaker has been the minister of petroleum and mineral
resources for Saudi Arabia since 1962, and this was an important statement of future
intent on the part of the oil producers. The need for change is seen because of the lack
of contact between the consumers and the producers, for which both parties, in
addition to the oil companies, were equally responsible. The lecture is a reasoned
examination of the problem and seeks to explore and define the new relationship,
which is seen as direct contact between the producer and the consumer with 'the role
being played by the oil companies now...that of a purchaser, refiner and provider of
technology'.

602 **Yamani tempts U.S. with vast oil deal.**
Oil and Gas Journal, vol. 70 (1972), p. 35-7.

A proposal from the Saudi Arabian oil minister that the Americans should be allowed
quota-free shipments of crude oil, in return for Saudi Arabia being allowed to make
large investments in U.S. oil facilities.

March arabesque.
See item no. 31.

Economic geography of Islamic countries.
See item no. 498.

The economies of the Arab world: development since 1945.
See item no. 526.

Saudi Arabian development strategy.
See item no. 564.

Aspects of Saudi Arabia through the ages.
See item no. 740.

Oil as an economic and political weapon

603 **The oil crisis: this time the wolf is here.**
James E. Akins. *Foreign Affairs*, vol. 51, pt. 3 (1973), p. 462-90.

tAn interesting article which looks at the global energy requirements and oil reserves, and concludes that the pessimistic forecasts are based on facts, with the world approaching a crisis. The article is general in coverage, but consideration is given to the Arab world in depth and especially to Saudi Arabia because of its proven reserves. The particular problem raised is the possibility of oil being used as a political weapon, and the likely effects when so much dependence is placed on imports from the Middle East.

604 **Saudi Arabia and oil diplomacy.**
Rustum Sheikh Ali. New York, London: Praeger, 1976. 197p. maps. bibliog.

605 **Why OPEC will watch the Western summit.**
Malcolm Brown. *The Times* (London), (16 June 1978), p. 27.

A consideration of the pricing of oil in relation to the dollar situation, which examines Saudi Arabia's role as a moderating influence within the organization.

606 **Oil revenues and industrialization in the Arab oil-producing countries.**
Nimr Eid, Edward Armaly. *Industrial Marketing Management*, vol. 4, pt. 1 (1974), p. 9-13.

Saudi Arabia is considered, together with the other states, with regard to the unprecedented investment management problems: 1. To what extent can the states absorb capital inflows? 2. What are the economic implications for the industrialized world? 3. What are the ramifications for the international monetary system?

607 **OPEC keeps its balance.**
P. E. L. Fellowes. *Middle East International*, (Feb. 1977), p. 8-11.

A discussion of the 1976 OPEC pricing meeting, which resulted in a pricing differential between Saudi Arabia and the United Arab Emirates and the other eleven producers. The author considers the implications of this action, the motives for the stand taken by Saudi Arabia, and the prospects for the future.

608 **OPEC and the price freeze.**
Adrian D. Hamilton. *Middle East International*, (Feb. 1978), p. 12-14.

Following the meeting of OPEC in December 1977 and further restraint of prices, the author discusses the position of Saudi Arabia as a critical factor in the oil economy. In

125

particular he examines the alliance between Saudi Arabia and the USA, which was rendered even more powerful by the alignment of Iranian interests. 'Once the Iranians and the Saudis had got together, the other producing countries were powerless....This triangle is likely to remain the decisive factor in oil politics for some time to come'.

609 The great oil sheikhdam.
Stephen D. Krasner. *Foreign Policy*, no. 13, vol. 3 (1973-74), p. 123-38.

A discussion of the implications of the use of oil as a political weapon, especially in relation to the question of Israel. The author argues that the weapon cannot be exchanged for political power, and that the problem is complicated by the international oil companies.

610 Probing the Arab motivation behind use of the oil weapon.
George Lenczowski. *International Perspectives*, (March-April 1974), p. 3-9.

The oil states decided in October 1973 to use oil as a means of achieving their foreign policy, beginning with a 10 per cent cut in production from the September levels, with further monthly cuts in output. In addition the posted prices were also raised, and some countries were designated as unfriendly and were denied Arab oil completely. The main reason for the success of this particular operation was the fact that at this time the producers were in a sellers' market, with insufficient alternative supplies and a steadily increasing demand, especially in the United States which moved from self-sufficiency to partial dependence on imports. The consumer nations were divided into four categories - most favoured, friendly nations, other nations and embargoed nations. The motivations were also considered to be four in number - 'conservation concern for a depletable resource, adjustment of influx of funds to a limited absorptive capacity of certain producing countries, maximization of profits, and use of oil as a political weapon'.

611 The community of oil exporting countries: a study in governmental co-operation.
Zuhayr Mikdashi. Ithaca, New York; London: Cornell University Press, 1972. 218p. bibliog.

A study of the formation and development of OPEC, valuable for its examination of the co-operation between the various member states with regard to the pricing of oil, levels of production, etc.

612 The monetary edge of the oil weapon.
Banker, vol. 48 (March 1974), p. 253-71.

This survey examines the impact of oil price rises on the world economy, and the use of oil as a political weapon. Also considered are the sizes of the surpluses of the producing nations, and the ways in which these funds will be used. The survey covers the following topics: The monetary edge of the oil weapon; How the oil companies pay for the oil; Oil and money - your questions answered; Plans for deploying surpluses in the developing world; Bankers troop to the Middle East; Country survey.

613 OPEC: Two years on.
The Economist, (20 Sept. 1975), p. 13-14.

An assessment of OPEC two years after the price rises of 1973, which considers the role played by the Arab world in the world oil market and the reactions of the Western world toward the Arabs. The point is made that the moderate leaders, especially in Saudi Arabia, 'are men that Western politicians know they must help and benefit from, for there are unlikely to be better; any more dangerous Arabs in their place would now have the power to make the world more dangerous than Nasser ever made it'.

614 Saudi Arabia: a nation we'd better get to know.
Forbes Magazine, (15 Feb. 1973), p. 28-42.

Discusses the significance of Saudi Arabia, in the light of her economic and political power resulting from the world oil supply situation, and the use of oil as a weapon.

615 The Middle East, oil and the great powers.
Benjamin Shwadran.   New Brunswick, New Jersey: Transaction Books, 1973; Tel Aviv: Israel University Press, 1974. 3rd ed. 500p. maps.

Discusses the role of oil in relation to power politics in the Middle East.

March arabesque.
See item no. 31.

Imperialism and nationalism in the fertile crescent: sources and prospects of the Arab-Israeli conflict.
See item no. 303.

Confrontation: the Middle East war and world politics.
See item no. 344.

Beyond the energy crisis.
See item no. 548.

Middle East oil in a revolutionary age.
See item no. 588.

Petroleum politics, 1951-1974: a five-act drama reconstructed.
See item no. 598.

Industrial
Diversification

616 **Reducing dependence on oil.**
Tony Aldous. *The Times* (London), (28 Sept. 1970), p. V.
An account of the programme planned in order to achieve industrial diversification.

617 **The role of the College of Petroleum and Minerals in the industrialization of Saudi Arabia.**
Saleh Ambah. In: *Science and technology in developing countries.* Edited by Claire Nader and A. B. Zahlan. Cambridge, New York: Cambridge University Press, 1969, p. 249-71.

618 **Arabs and their oil.**
Earl V. Anderson. *Chemical and Engineering News*, (Nov. 1970), p. 58-72.
Concerned solely with the possible role of the Arab world in the field of petrochemicals, examining the world market for these products, and the increasingly significant role that the Arab world will play in the future in supplying them within the Arab World and to the industrialized nations.

619 **The Arab iron and steel industry.**
Arab Economist, no. 66, vol. 6 (July 1974), p. 42-9.
A report from the Arab Iron and Steel Union which has been abstracted to provide an accurate view about the actual conditions prevailing in this industry. The article is supported by reproduction of several of the statistical tables relating to production, thus enabling useful comparisons to be made between Saudi Arabia and the other Arab producers.

620 **Industry: ambitious plans.**

N. E. Bouari. *Arab Economist*, no. 65, vol. 6 (June 1974), p. 34-44.

Industrial plans for major development are scheduled in the five-year plan, and these are considered in this contribution to a special supplement on Saudi Arabia in the light of government policy. The problems are also discussed, especially those of manpower shortages, size of market and underutilization of capacity. The author concludes by examining possible future achievements, especially in the field of petrochemicals but also in other areas, possibly in partnership with other Arab countries. Detailed consideration is also given to the role of incentives as a means of both improving efficiency and promoting exports, and of improving the quality of domestically produced goods.

621 **Marine industries of eastern Arabia.**

Richard Le Baron Bowen. *Geographical Review*, vol. 41, pt. 3 (1951), p. 384-400. maps.

An examination of the coastal towns of the Arabian Gulf coast of Saudi Arabia, dealing with the means of existence of their inhabitants. The author deals with fishing and the methods of fishing, including the use of fish weirs, rock mining for dead coral, and pearling. He makes the point that these traditional occupations were on the decline, due to the higher wages offered by the oil companies, though the situation in Saudi Arabia was not as critical as elsewhere in the Gulf.

622 **Operation Bultiste: promoting industrial development in Saudi Arabia.**

Carleton Stevens Coon. In: *Hands across frontiers: case studies in technical co-operation.* Edited by H. M. Teaf and P. G. Frank. Ithaca, New York: Cornell University Press, 1955, p. 307-61.

623 **Construction and equipment in the Arab world.**

The Times (London), (17 Oct. 1977), 14p.

A special report which presents an examination of the construction programme in the Arab world, including Saudi Arabia, which spent $16,000 million on construction and development work in 1976, representing an increase of 34 per cent over the previous year.

624 **Planning industrial development in the Arab countries.**

F. R. Fahmi. *L'Egypte Contemporaine*, vol. 58 (April 1967), p. 31-2.

A survey of diversification programmes in the Arab world, including Saudi Arabia.

625 **Jeddah's steel rolling mill.**

Arab World, no. 26 (1970), p. 13-14.

A brief account of the steel rolling mill in Jeddah, which is a move toward industrial diversification, and an attempt to reduce the Saudis' dependence upon imported steel for the construction industry.

Industrial Diversification

626 **Industrialization in the Middle East: obstacles and potential.**
Ragasi el-Mallakh. *Middle East Studies Association Bulletin*,
vol. 7, pt. 3 (1973), p. 28-46.

Discussion of the whole of the Middle East, with general considerations, studies by
country, and a regional assessment. One problem highlighted by the author is that 'the
needed research for sustained industrial development has lagged behind the desire for
and interest in that sector, and such research and literature are still in only the
beginning phases'.

627 **Science and technology in developing countries.**
Edited by Claire Nader, A. B. Zahlan. London, New York:
Cambridge University Press, 1969. 588p.

Proceedings of a conference held at the American University of Beirut, 27
November-2 December 1967.

628 **Saudi Arabia broadens industrial base.**
World Petroleum, vol. 39 (1968), p. 24-6.

A description of plans to diversify industrial operations to reduce dependence on oil
revenues.

629 **Regional plan of action for the application of science and
technology to development in the Middle East.**
United Nations. New York: United Nations, 1974. 107p.

Saudi Arabia.
See item no. 153.

Saudi Arabia today.
See item no. 460.

Administrative reform in Saudi Arabia.
See item no. 482.

Saudi Arabia 2000: a strategy for growth.
See item no. 496.

Economic report: Saudi Arabia.
See item no. 500.

The economies of the Arab world: development since 1945.
See item no. 526.

Minerals and Mining

630 **Notes on the mineral resources of the Middle East.**
J. D. Boyd, R. Duncan.   Cairo: Middle East Supply Centre, 1945.

631 **Mineral reconnaissance of the al-Zizl quadrangle, northwest Hijaz.**
R. F. Johnson, V. A. Trent.   Jeddah: Ministry of Petroleum and Mineral Resources, 1967.

632 **Mineral reconnaissance of the Qalet as Sawrak quadrangle.**
R. F. Johnson, V. A. Trent.   Jeddah: Ministry of Petroleum and Mineral Resources, 1967.

633 **Reconnaisance investigations in the Jabal al Lavz quadrangle, Aqaba area.**
R. F. Johnson, V. A. Trent.   Jeddah: Ministry of Petroleum and Mineral Resources, 1967.

634 **Reconnaisance, mineral and geologic investigations in the Hagl quadrangle, Aqaba area.**
R. F. Johnson, V. A. Trent.   Jeddah: Ministry of Petroleum and Mineral Resources, 1967.

Minerals and Mining

635 Saudi Arabia's exploration program reveals significant mineral finds.
F. Kabbani. *Engineering Mining Journal*, vol. 167, pt. 4 (1966), p. 89-98.

A detailed study of the results of the government-sponsored exploration to ascertain the reserves of minerals other than oil, and their potential for exploitation.

636 Saudi Arabia minerals.
Mining Journal, no. 6654, vol. 260 (1963), p. 202.

A survey of the mineral potential of Saudi Arabia.

637 Saudi Arabia's industrial future.
Middle East International, (July 1978), p. 18-20.

An inverview with Dr. Ghazi Abdul-Rahman al-Gasaibi, Saudi Arabia's minister of industry and electricity, concerning the diversification programme aimed at supplementing revenues in the 1980s. The main centres are to be at Yenbo on the Red Sea and Jubail on the Arabian Gulf, using gas as a source of energy, and concentrating on hydro-carbon processing and mineral smelting.

638 Saudi Arabia's new mineral development programme.
Engineering Mining Journal, vol. 166, pt. 11 (1965), p. 87-96.

The programme for diversification into the exploitation of minerals, other than oil, to broaden the base of the economy.

639 Much to do before minerals can be tapped.
Pearce Wright. *The Times* (London), (23 Sept. 1976), p. VIII.

Special report which discusses the problems to be faced before Saudi Arabia can exploit mineral resources on a commercial basis.

Economic report: Saudi Arabia.
See item no. 500.

The economies of the Arab world: development since 1945.
See item no. 526.

Middle East oil money and its future expenditure.
See item no. 586.

Foreign investment in the petroleum and mineral industries; case studies of investor-host country relations.
See item no. 595.

Agriculture

640 **Anglo-Arabian shrimp fishing venture in the Persian Gulf.**
Commercial Fisheries Review, vol. 27, pt. 3 (1965), p. 87.
An account of British involvement in the modernization of fishing methods in the eastern province.

641 **A fattening trial with yearling rams of the Saudi Arabian Najdi and Arabi breeds.**
H. Appleman. *Netherlands Journal of Agricultural Science*, vol. 18, pt. 1 (1970), p. 84-8.
An account of a fattening trial on yearling rams conducted at the Qatif Experimental Farm, near Dammam, which produced inconclusive results due to the variability between the individual animals and the small numbers used, i.e. eight of each breed. The data collected, however, should be of interest for further research in the field.

642 **Saudi Arabia: long-term projections of supply of a demand for agricultural products.**
Edmond Y. Asfour (and others). Beirut: American University of Beirut. Economic Research Institute, 1965. 180p. bibliog.
Agricultural activity in Saudi Arabia is predominantly occupied with the supply of food. No crop other than animal feed is produced in any significant quantity for use in non-food industries. However, some animals, such as camels and horses, are raised for purposes of transportation, draft, and selective breeding. Agriculture and animal husbandry in Saudi Arabia are subsistence activities. The greater part of their output is consumed by the farmers and Bedouins themselves, and little surplus is available for sale. Due to the isolation of most of the many small production areas, a large part of agricultural output does not enter the money market, and production for sale, except near the cities, is of small significance. The backwardness of agriculture is essentially due to the intemperate climate and the scarcity of resources, particularly water. The cultivated area, estimated at 245,000 hectares, is only about 0.13 per cent of the total land of the country.

Agriculture

643 Agrarian reform policies and development in the Arab world.

F. Baali. *American Journal of Economics and Sociology*, vol. 33, pt. 2 (1974), p. 161-74.

The section on Saudi Arabia (p. 164-5) deals only with developments since 1960, and these only in brief outline. The introductory section deals mainly with all other countries except Saudi Arabia, but the concluding section dealing with the evaluation of the present state of development is of relevance.

644 Agricultural potential of the Middle East.

Marion Clawson (and others). New York, London: Elsevier, 1971. 315p.

The authors considered that little accurate data was available about the agriculture of Saudi Arabia, with the result 'that in many of the tables and much of the discussion in the main part of this book, it was not considered possible to consider Saudi Arabia on the same basis as the other countries'. Hence treatment of Saudi Arabia is in the form of a short appendix, p. 298-300, which does however provide a useful survey of the agricultural potential of the country.

645 Recent agricultural developments in Saudi Arabia.

Douglas D. Crary. *Geographical Review*, vol. 41, pt. 3 (1951), p. 366-83. maps.

A study of the use made of oil to increase agricultural production within definite geographical limitations. The point is strongly made that the new methods relate only to mechanization, the use of fertilizers, and seed selection, as the basic principles of irrigated agriculture have been followed in Arabia for over 2000 years. Also, although advances are being made, the deserts of Arabia are not suddenly going to become rich agricultural land, as the costs involved are enormous and the difficulties very real. The author considers the al Kharj project, which is some fifty-five miles southeast of Riyadh, dealing with the background to the project, the economics, and the agricultural limitations. Also described is the Hafuf project, which is at the al Hasa oasis, and which has a large population and an adequate supply of water.

646 Dates: handling, processing and packing.

V. H. W. Dawson, A. Aten. Rome: Food and Agriculture Organization, 1962. (Agricultural Development Paper, no. 77).

647 Utilization and human geography of the deserts.

J. Dresch. *Transactions of the Institute of British Geographers*, vol. 40 (1966), p. 1-10.

Refers to the Middle East in general terms. Of particular relevance is the discussion of the decline of nomadism, the evolution of agriculture, and the conditions of settlement.

648 Fishing in Arabia.
Donald S. Erdman. *Scientific Monthly*, vol. 70, pt. 1 (1950),
p. 58-65. map.

A description of the fishing industry of the Arabian Gulf, with details of the various
fish caught, the nature of the communities, and the weather and tides of the Gulf.
Also described is the fishing available at the oasis of al Hasa, and the various
communities there which, in spite of modernization, still observe the customs of
centuries.

649 A greening in the Arab east.
Joseph Fitchett. *Aramco World* , vol. 23, pt. 6 (1972), p.
24-33.

Discusses the work of the Arid Lands Agricultural Development Program to encourage
improved water management, and farming technology. Detailed consideration is given
to the question of wheat, because of its importance as a food crop in the Middle East,
and there is discussion of the development of various strains, especially those that can
survive in 'the vast, unirrigated, but rainfed areas where the Middle East's poorest
farmers work, and from which more and more of the area's wheat will have to come
as increased demand for luxury crops pushes wheat out of irrigated areas'.

650 Report to the government of Saudi Arabia on grazing resources and problems.
Harold F. Heady. Rome: Food and Agriculture Organization,
1963. (ETAP Report no. 1614, Project SAU/TE/PL).

651 Report to the government of Saudi Arabia: pasture development and range management.
Marvin Klemme. Rome: Food and Agriculture Organization,
1965. (Report no. 1993).

652 Characteristics and problems of agriculture in Saudi Arabia.
N. A. Lateef. Rome: Food and Agriculture Organization,
1956. (Background Country Study, no. 4).

653 Hasa: an Arabian oasis.
J. B. Mackie. *Geographical Journal*, vol. 63, pt. 3 (1924), p.
189-207.

A description of the al Hasa oasis giving details of the various settlements, the
agriculture and the method of administration through the Amir. A considerable part of
the article is devoted to a discussion of the irrigation of the area, and to a comparison
between al Hasa and the cultivated areas around Basra in Iraq.

Agriculture

654 Agricultural production in Saudi Arabia (1380-1383AH).
G. S. Medawar. Beirut: American University of Beirut.
Economic Research Institute, 1964.

655 Saudi Arabia: supply and demand projections for farm products to 1975, with implications for U.S. exports.
L. E. Moe. Washington, D.C.: U.S. Dept. of Agriculture, 1966.

Examines the likely agricultural output and the likely requirements, measuring these projections against the possible market for U.S. machinery, fertilizers and experience.

656 Saudi Arabia targets vast sums for development.
John B. Parker. *Foreign Agriculture*, vol. 13, pt. 20 (1975), p. 3-4, 7-14. map.

An examination of the need for Saudi Arabia to expand food production to keep pace with mounting needs and, in particular, of proposals for agriculture under the five-year plan. The point is made that even though investment may produce high levels of output, farm imports will still increase because 'a growing population and aspirations for a better life have created an unprecedented demand for more and better food'. The author considers the advance of new technology, government support for farmers, and education and training. Also of importance is the money being invested in irrigation which, in 1975, represented the means of supplying water to about one-fifth of the area under cultivation, mainly from underground sources. Developments are taking place to use trapped rainwater and to build desalination plants, especially in the area bordering on the Gulf.

657 U.S. farm exports benefit as Saudi Arabia's oil income soars.
John B. Parker. *Foreign Agriculture*, vol. 12, pt. 17 (1974), p. 2-5, 9.

Saudi Arabia imports one-third of its food, and the author discusses the effect that this, together with a change in eating patterns, is having on the exports of the United States. He also discusses the agricultural development programmes being undertaken in Saudi Arabia, and the effects that these are likely to have on requirements for agricultural products. The article is illustrated and has statistical tables of U.S. agricultural exports to Saudi Arabia from 1963/64 to 1973/74, Saudi Arabian grain supply from 1969 to 1974, and total agricultural imports from 1963 to 1974.

658 Saudi agriculture.
Ramzi Saab. *Arab Economist*, no. 65, vol. 6 (June 1974), p. 51-3.

A contribution to a special supplement on Saudi Arabia. The place of agriculture in Saudi Arabia is largely determined by topography and climate, and for many years revolved around sheep and camels. A programme of agricultural development has been put into operation, with improved methods of irrigation, and increases in the water supply by construction of dams and drilling of wells. The author considers in conclusion important developments for the future: farmer education, the eradication improvements, with farmer education being important, the eradication of desert locusts, and sand stabilization. Also the fishing industry should be profitably exploited, and the use of hydroponics considered to maximize production with limited water supplies.

659 Co-operative development in the kingdom of Saudi Arabia.
Ghazi Sabbagh. *Yearbook of Agricultural Co-operation*, (1972), p. 109-15.

The co-operative movement in Saudi Arabia was ten years old in 1972, and is successful because 'the idea springs from the very roots of the community's religious and social traditions' and is sustained by government support. The main co-operatives are examined, as are the laws, rules and administration necessary to support the movement and to allow for education and training, mainly in the rural areas.

660 Processing of dates in the eastern province of Saudi Arabia.
Z. I. Sabry.   Beirut: American University of Beirut. Agricultural Science Faculty, 1960.

661 Science and technology in the eastern Arab countries.
Princeton, New Jersey: Seventeenth Near East Conference, 1965. 63p.

Amongst papers presented were: 'Applicability of desalting process in the arid zones', by J. Ricca; 'Saudi Arabia and petroleum technology', by G. Rentz.

662 Shrimp fishing in the Persian Gulf expanding.
Commercial Fisheries Review, vol. 21, pt. 7 (1959), p. 68-9.

663 Development of irrigation farms, with special reference to irrigation and crop production under desert conditions, as observed in Saudi Arabia.
J. T. Smith.   In: *Proceedings of the United Nations Scientific Conference on Conservation and Utilization of Resources, New York*, vol. 4, 1951, p. 385-8.

664 Research on agricultural development in selected Middle East countries.
Donald C. Taylor.   New York: Agricultural Development Council, 1968. 166p.

Section on Saudi Arabia: p. 104-9.

Agriculture

665 Agrarian reform and urbanization in the Middle East.
Elias H. Tuma. *Middle East Journal*, vol. 24 (1970), p. 163-77.

Discusses the changes in the traditional patterns of agriculture and land tenure, and the moves towards an urban society.

666 Population, food and agriculture in the Arab countries.
Elias H. Tuma. *Middle East Journal*, vol. 28, pt. 3 (1974), p. 381-95.

The author discusses the relationship between population growth and agricultural output, dealing with the interdependence of the two factors, and the prevailing conditions in Arab countries. The policies relating to population control and family planning are also considered, as are the policies affecting agriculture and its ability to maintain a viable balance with demographic change. The final section proposes priority areas for research and policy implementation in an area where the potential for vast improvement exists. As this deals with the Arab world as a whole, the material relating to Saudi Arabia, except for the statistics, can only be drawn from a complete reading of the article.

667 Date culture in the oasis of al-Hasa.
Frederico S. Vidal. *Middle East Journal*, vol. 8, pt. 4 (1954), p. 417-28.

A study of the life and work of the Saudi Arabians along the Arabian Gulf by an American anthropologist.

668 Arabian locust hunter.
G. F. Walford. London: Hale, 1963. 176p. maps.

An account of the work of the anti-locust unit operating in the Arabian peninsula in an attempt to eradicate the locust and prevent the periodic destruction of crops.

Saudi Arabia.
See item no. 7.

The Middle East: a handbook.
See item no. 24.

The Middle East: a geographical study.
See item no. 142.

Saudi Arabia.
See item no. 153.

Saudi Arabia offers a rich potential of water development.
See item no. 161.

Water resources and irrigation development in the Middle East.
See item no. 178.

A dam in Saudi Arabia.
See item no. 179.

The Bedouin.
See item no. 383.

The nomad problem and the implementation of a nomadic settlement scheme in Saudi Arabia.
See item no. 426.

Saudi Arabia today.
See item no. 460.

Administrative reform in Saudi Arabia.
See item no. 482.

Riyadh and the central province.
See item no. 518.

Saudi Arabia: investment opportunities.
See item no. 521.

The economies of the Arab world: development since 1945.
See item no. 526.

Requiem for the empty quarter.
See item no. 576.

Middle East oil money and its future expenditure.
See item no. 586.

Urbanization

669 Urbanization in the Middle East.
V. F. Costello. London, New York: Cambridge University Press, 1977. 121p. map. bibliog.

Urbanization is considered in relation to the region as a whole, with references to Saudi Arabia interspersed throughout the text. The work deals with the Middle East environment and the pre-urban society, before considering urban development. The subject of modern urban development is dealt with by examining rural-urban migration, the problems of social adjustment, occupations and social strata, and the structure and form of urban development.

670 Model houses for el Dareeya, Saudi Arabia.
Hassan Fathy. *Ekistics*, no. 124, vol. 21 (1966), p. 214-19.

A description of the designs of local model houses at el Dareeya which were prepared to meet the following requirements: 1. Needs of modern life; 2. Preservation of the Arabic architectural style; 3. Use of local building materials; 4. Respect for inherited traditions and customs; 5. Improvements in design and construction; 6. Provision for natural temperature control - without the use of foreign equipment. The principles applied and the solutions chosen are illustrated by a comparison of the architecture of the old houses, and that of the developed models.

671 The nature of Islamic urbanization: an historical perspective.
Riaz Hassan. *Islamic Culture*, vol. 43 (1969), p. 233-7.

A discussion of the urbanization of pre-industrialized society which, although not directly concerned with Saudi Arabia, is of relevance. The author presents the idea that any study of Islamic urbanization must be linked to a study of Islamic religious tradition 'for certain features of religious tradition of Islam are underlying factors in the evaluation of Muslim urbanization'. As Saudi Arabia is a society based very much on Islamic tradition this article is obviously of significance.

672 **Jeddah 68/69: the first and only definitive introduction to Jeddah, Saudi Arabia's most modern and varied city.**
Nairobi: University Press of Arabia, 1968. 174p. maps.
A guidebook to Jeddah, the third most important city in Saudi Arabia, with information on shopping, hotels, embassies, government departments, industry, etc.

673 **Housing in Saudi Arabia and the Arab countries of the Gulf.**
Abdul Latif Kanoo. London: Longman, 1978. 240p.
Examines the various problems associated with providing housing, in particular the problems of topography and social structures, and discusses the variety of materials and structures used to solve these problems. The author also describes the types of houses and methods of building used in the past, and those currently used, as well as the relevant economic factors.

674 **Jiddah: portrait of an Arabian city.**
Angelo Pesce. London: Falcon Press, 1977. Rev. ed. 239p. maps.
A comprehensive, well-written study of the traditional commercial centre of Saudi Arabia. This book is really a study of the evolution of Jeddah, but the depth of coverage is such that it is also important for the historical, social, economic, and environmental aspects. The author has divided his study into five basic sections, with additional sections containing coloured plates and statistical appendices: 1. Western Arabia in antiquity; 2. Jeddah in the Arabic geographic literature of the classic period; 3. Jeddah in the accounts of travellers and explorers from the 11th to the 19th century; 4. Historical background; 5. Contemporary Jeddah.

675 **Riyadh: history and guide.**
William Pugh. Dammam, Saudi Arabia: al Mutair Press, 1969. 112p. maps.
A brief historical survey of the development of Riyadh into the capital of Saudi Arabia, and a guide book to the city and its environs.

676 **Social trends in Arab cities.**
I. Qutub. *Middle East Forum*, vol. 40, pt. 1 (1964), p. 25-8.
Discusses the effects of urbanism on the social structure.

677 **The face of Medina.**
F. Rayess. *Aramco World*, vol. 16, pt. 6 (1965), p. 12-15.
A description of one of the holy cities of Islam.

678 **Saudi Arabia: master plan for the city of Riyadh.**
Doxiadis Associates Review, no. 43, vol. 4 (1968), p. 1-8.
A detailed examination of the plan proposed for the creation of the new city.

Urbanization

679 Saudi Arabia: preliminary plan for Riyadh approved.
Doxiadis Associates Review, no. 57, vol. 5 (1969), p. 7-8.
An outline of the plan to develop Riyadh as part of a controlled development programme.

680 Saudi Arabia: Riyadh master plan.
Doxiadis Associates Review, no. 45, vol. 4 (1968), p. 7-9.
An outline of the plan produced to ensure controlled development of Riyadh.

681 Saudi Arabia: Riyadh preliminary plan.
Doxiadis Associates Review, no. 53, vol. 5 (1969), p. 7-8.
An outline of the first draft of the development plan for Riyadh.

682 Recent Arab city growth.
Saba George Shiber. Kuwait: Kuwait Government Printing Press, 1969. 832p.
The author was a leading Arab planner until his death in 1969. This work is a collection of studies on urban planning and growth which originally appeared in the Kuwaiti and Lebanese press. Saudi Arabia is included in the collection, and development there is criticized, as it is in the rest of the Arab world, for its addiction to showmanship and prestige, with little regard to the real needs of the population.

Some geographical aspects of al Riyadh.
See item no. 138.

Fertility patterns and their determinants in the Arab Middle East.
See item no. 423.

Jiddah and the western province.
See item no. 511.

Agrarian reform and urbanization in the Middle East.
See item no. 665.

Educational problems of Arab countries.
See item no. 735.

Transport, Communications and Trade

683 Domestic air passenger transport in Saudi Arabia.
Assad S. Abdo. *Bulletin of the Faculty of Arts, University of Riyadh*, vol. 1 (1970), p. 21-39.

A survey of the development of domestic airline communications in Saudi Arabia, tracing their growth from the earliest beginnings.

684 The evolution of modern roads in Saudi Arabia.
Assad S Abdo. *Bulletin de la Société de Géographie d'Egypte*, vol. 41, pt. 2 (1968), p. 23-42. maps.

A survey of the development of a modern road system in Saudi Arabia, treating roads as 'a product of human activities built to serve certain requirements of life'. The author concludes that the road system grew according to the same pattern as the socio-economic development of Saudi Arabia, and that the road system is closely related to the exploitation and the growth of the government budget.

685 Road traffic in Saudi Arabia.
Assad S. Abdo. *Bulletin of the Faculty of Arts, University of Riyadh*, vol. 2 (1971-72), p. 77-95.

A detailed examination of the growth of road traffic in Saudi Arabia in relation to the road building programme, with reference to the need of the economy to secure an effective communications network.

Transport, Communications and Trade

686 Saudi Arabia.
M. S. Ahmed. New York: Chase World Information
Corporation, 1977. 375p. maps.

This work is one of a series of market intelligence publications, designed to provide
the businessman with information for marketing and investment.

687 Middle East international highways from caravan routes to modern roads.
M. S. Ahmad. *Middle East Journal*, vol. 21 (1967), p. 101-7.

Transport routes in the Middle East are seen as an important subject, because of the
outstanding part played by the Arabian peninsula in the development of civilization in
many parts of the world. A great deal of the article is therefore devoted to the early
movements of peoples within the region, and the development of recognized caravan
and trading routes. This leads to a consideration of present-day developments in
communications which have been dictated by trading requirements, the need to develop industry, and the growth of agriculture. 'After the existing roads are linked with
the adjoining countries...the old caravan routes will be reopened and an ancient dream
will be recaptured. Such is the persistent cycle of history'.

688 Warm welcome for Britain.
Tim Albert. *Observer* (London), (11 July 1976), p. 26.

Stresses that the Saudi Arabian market is growing, and that British firms have the
advantage of being welcomed by the Saudi Arabian government.

689 British exporters eye Saudi boom.
Gerald Butt. *Arab World*, no. 37 (1973), p. 8-11.

A study of the Saudi Arabian market potential which exists as a result of the income
from oil, and the attraction that this holds for British exports.

690 Foreign trade of the Middle East: instability and growth, 1946-62.
Joseph David Coppock. Beirut: American University of Beirut.
Economic Research Institute, 1966.

This work is concerned with the fluctuation of exports and imports in nine countries
including Saudi Arabia. Little comparison is made between the countries in question,
and the work consists mainly of tables and diagrams covering goods, services and
potential growth trends.

691 Winning business in Saudi Arabia.
Nicholas Fallon. London: Graham & Trotman, 1976. 61p.
maps.

This work is mainly designed for the businessman seeking to export to Saudi Arabia.
It offers advice on methods of operation, market potential, etc.

692 Inland freight transportation pricing in eastern Saudi Arabia.

R. N. Farmer. *Journal of Industrial Economics*, vol. 10, pt. 3 (1962), p. 174-87.

In considering the pricing of transportation, the author deals first with the economic background to the region and the structure of the transport system. He then examines the structure of the market and the cost factors relating to the operation of inland freight movements. The last section of the 'article deals with the fixing of prices; these are determined locally by oral bargaining, and vary radically according to the state of demand. In addition, Aramco operates its own tariff based on the American system, and the American pricing structure also operates for the railway.

693 The great freight race.

The Times (London), (28 Oct. 1977), p. I-VIII.

A special report dealing with the solutions adopted by exporters to satisfy orders from the Middle East, particularly with regard to the necessity to meet delivery dates.

694 The future of the north Arabian desert.

A. L. Holt. *Geographical Journal*, vol. 62 (1923), p. 259-71.

This article resulted from a journey undertaken in company with St. John Philby to Jauf, but is concerned solely with the potential of the area as a line of communication, and as an important trade route.

695 Pilgrim's airport.

Ian Macdowell. *Arab World*, no. 22 (Summer 1969), p. 11.

An account of the operation and development of Jeddah airport, and the problems of coping with the traffic for the Hajj.

696 The Hejaz railroad.

S. McLoughlin. *Geographical Journal*, vol. 124, pt. 2 (1958), p. 282-3.

A series of notes on the state of the Hedjaz railway and the various stations, resulting from a visit in 1957. Interesting in the light of proposals aimed at reopening the railway for pilgrim and trade traffic from Damascus.

697 The Hedjaz railway.

F. R. Maunsell. *Geographical Journal*, vol. 32, pt. 6 (1908), p. 570-85. map.

The Hedjaz railway was built to provide improved access to the holy places, and also to facilitate greater central oversight of the outlying provinces of the Ottoman empire. This article describes the various stages of the construction of the railway, the operating difficulties, and the topography of the surrounding area.

698 Saudi Arabia, business opportunities.

Metra Consulting Group Ltd. London: The Financial Times, 1975. 189p. maps.

A market intelligence publication specifically designed for companies with an interest in marketing in Saudi Arabia.

Transport, Communications and Trade

699 Near East, South Asia: real trade role seen as vastly increased oil revenues boost demand.
Commerce Today, vol. 4, pt. 21 (1974), p. 36-42.

700 The highways of central Arabia.
H. St. John B. Philby. *Journal of the Royal Central Asian Society*, vol. 7 (1920), p. 112.

701 Record trade role seen in Near East-South Asia.
Commerce Today, vol. 4 (July 1974), p. 36-42.

Examines American trade with the Middle East as increased oil revenues boost the demand for imported goods. Saudi Arabia is dealt with specifically on page 39, with statistical data on imports from the United States as well as information on the openings available for technical expertise to take advantage of 'one of the world's most massive sustained programs of construction and industrialization'.

702 Flying in the major airline league.
Arthur Reed. ·*The Times* (London), (24 Sept. 1976), p. IV.

An account of the growth of Saudia Airways as a major carrier of passengers and freight on international routes.

703 Saudi Arabia ready for giant tanker era.
World Petroleum, vol. 40 (1969), p. 22-4.

Outlines the improvements made to harbour and loading facilities in preparation for the use of supertankers.

704 Saudi Arabia: rich field for exporters.
Middle East Economic Digest, vol. 17, pt. 4 (1973), p. 87-90.

Outlines the potential of the booming Saudi Arabian economy.

705 Saudi Arabia: sources of imports and direction of exports.
Arab Economist, no. 51, vol. 5 (April 1973), p. 73-4.

An overview of the pattern of Saudi Arabian trade; includes statistics.

706 4,000M dollars plan to improve ports.
David Shirreff. *The Times* (London), (24 Sept. 1976), p. IV.

A special report presenting an account of the development plan aimed at improving port facilities in order to reduce the time spent by ships waiting to unload vital raw materials.

707 Road building will treble by 1980.
David Shirreff. *The Times* (London), (24 Sept. 1976), p. XI.

A special report which examines the road development programme, a vital element in unifying the kingdom, improving communications, and facilitating internal commerce.

708 **The Hedjaz railway: pilgrim trains to run again.**
N. Tannus. *Arab World*, vol. 4 (1964), p. 19-24.
The plan to repair and reopen the Hedjaz railway, mainly to facilitate the transportation of pilgrims.

709 **Aviation in the Arab world: problems and prospects.**
A. Tawil. *Arab Economist*, vol. 6, pt. 5 (1974), p. 4-21.
Considers in general the expansion of Arab airlines, passenger and freight transport, airport facilities, and the Federation of Arab Travel Agents and other organizations.

710 **Some aspects of the Arab dhow trade.**
A. Villiers. *Middle East Journal*, vol. 2, pt. 4 (1948), p. 399-416.
Examines the dhow trade, with special emphasis on the vessels themselves.

Saudi Arabia.
See item no. 7.

Saudi Arabia.
See item no. 153.

The pilgrim railway.
See item no. 406.

The nomad problem and the implementation of a nomadic settlement scheme in Saudi Arabia.
See item no. 426.

Saudi Arabia today.
See item no. 460.

Economic report: Saudi Arabia.
See item no. 500.

Jiddah and the western province.
See item no. 511.

Saudi Arabia: investment opportunities.
See item no. 521.

The economies of the Arab world: development since 1945.
See item no. 526.

Middle East oil money and its future expenditure.
See item no. 586.

Employment

711 Training for development.
Frank A. Clements. *Middle East International*, no. 76 (Oct. 1976), p. 19-21.

Discusses the problems presented by lack of trained manpower in attempts to diversify in industry, especially in the field of petrochemicals. The educational advances and financial provisions in Saudi Arabia are considered, as is the need for more co-operation between industry and the technical and vocational schools to ensure the right technical training. The long-term problems of shortage of labour are also considered, and a case is made for some form of regional co-operation, as 'success will not be achieved unless the problems of trained manpower shortages and co-ordinated effort on a regional basis can be solved'.

712 Experience with an industrial research program in the social sciences.
H. R. Pauling. *Journal of Business*, vol. 34 (1961), p. 140-52.

An account of the industrial relations research programme of Aramco, and its contribution to the oil operations in Saudi Arabia. Relations with the work force and the other peoples in area of Aramco's operation were initially the cause of major problems, because of the difficulties of operating in a foreign country, the profound effect of Aramco policies as the largest employer, and the lack of data essential to the finding of solutions. The author discusses the implications of these problems and the manner in which Aramco, through the research programme, set out to solve them.

713 Labour separation in an underdeveloped area: Saudi Arabia.
H. C. Pauling. *American Journal of Economic Sociology*, vol. 23, pt. 4 (1964), p. 419-34.

Using Aramco as a case study, the author examines workers' adjustment to change, the effects of which are significant in influencing the content of work and the organizational environment in which the work is performed. Initially the company faced a high rate of staff turnover, and the author considers this was due to problems in adaptation by workers to the industrial environment. The rate declined as other employment opportunities became available, and this tends to confirm the hypothesis that turnover is 'a problem of social and psychological adjustment rather than a reflection of economic considerations'.

714 The labour situation in Saudi Arabia.

United States. Bureau of Labor Statistics. *Labor Development Abroad*, vol. 14 (8 Aug. 1969), p. 1-9.

An examination of the labour situation in Saudi Arabia which needs to be considered in relation to the following item, an article devoted to Aramco. Some general information is followed by an examination of the labour force in relation to population and the various sectors of employment. Also dealt with are the problems of unemployment and underemployment, and the shortage of skills, with the attendant complications for manpower planning. Conditions of work are examined at length in relation to the labour code, the legal framework which governs such conditions, and finally there is a consideration of the wage structure, about which little information was available, but it is concluded that the generally higher wage rates as compared to other Arab countries were due directly to the influence of the oil industry.

715 The labour situation in Saudi Arabia.

United States. Bureau of Labor Statistics. *Labor Development Abroad*, vol. 14 (9 Sept. 1969), p. 1-7.

Deals specifically with the labour pattern of Aramco and with the role of the company in Saudi Arabia's industrial development. Considers the labour force, its composition and performance, and in particular the Saudi Arab component of the labour force. Also dealt with are the education and training programmes of the company, the incentives offered to employees, and the stability of the work force. Lastly the article deals with the conditions of work, and produces tables detailing severance payments, sick leave, and permanent total disability benefits.

716 Labour law and practice in the kingdom of Saudi Arabia.

United States. Bureau of Labor Statistics. Washington, D.C.: U.S. Government Printing Office, 1973. 103p.

One of a series produced by the Bureau, designed to provide background material for the American businessman. This is a brief authoritative analysis of great relevance and interest.

717 The long-run employment prospects for Middle East labour.

R. J. Ward. *Middle East Journal*, vol. 24, pt. 2 (1970), p. 147-62.

An informed article dealing with what could become a pressing problem, not only related to economics, but possessing political and social overtones.

A house built on sand: a political economy of Saudi Arabia.
See item no. 447.

Saudi Arabia 2000: a strategy for growth.
See item no. 496.

National science and technology policies in the Arab states: present situation and future outlook.
See item no. 517.

The economies of the Arab world: development since 1945.
See item no. 526.

Oil and state in the Middle East.
See item no. 547.

Employment

Middle East oil money and its future expenditure.
See item no. 586.

Housing in Saudi Arabia and the Arab countries of the Gulf.
See item no. 673.

Statistics

718 **Petroleum statistical bulletin.**
Saudi Arabia. Ministry of Petroleum and Mineral
Resources. Riyadh: The Ministry, annual.
An extremely valuable publication, in both English and Arabic, giving a complete
picture of the petroleum industry in Saudi Arabia. It is divided into two sections: the
first consists of tables, and the second of maps and graphs.

719 **Annual report.**
Saudi Arabian Monetary Agency. Research and Statistics
Department. Jeddah, Saudi Arabia: The Agency, annual.
The annual report of the Agency is the official guide to the economic aspects of the
kingdom, and should be used in conjunction with the Agency's *Statistical Summary*,
which updates the figures. Aspects covered are as follows: (a) General economic
survey; (b) Public finance; (c) Oil developments; (d) Money and banking; (e) Foreign
trade - balance of payments; (f) Economic development - subdivided by area of
activity; (g) Statistical tables.

720 **Statistical summary.**
Saudi Arabian Monetary Agency. Research and Statistics
Department. Jeddah, Saudi Arabia: The Agency, twice yearly.
This summary largely consists of statistical data, but it is prefaced by an assessment of
the Saudi economy, finance and banking, and of such aspects as development projects.
The statistical tables are in the following areas: (a) Money and banking; (b) Public
finance; (c) Oil statistics; (d) International transactions; (e) Prices and production; (f)
National accounts; (g) Pilgrimage.

721 **Demographic yearbook.**
United Nations. Statistical Office. New York: United Nations,
1948- , annual.
A comprehensive publication covering basic social statistics, such as population
growth rates, death rates, natality, and density.

Statistics

722 Statistical yearbook.
United Nations. Statistical Office.   New York: United Nations, 1948- , annual.

Subjects covered include communications, education, medicine, food production, and energy. Sources of data are given, as are notes to explain compilation and interpretation.

723 Yearbook of national accounts statistics.
United Nations. Statistical Office.   New York: United Nations, 1957- , annual.

Replaces *Statistics of national income and expenditure*, which appeared between 1938 and 1950. Covers aspects such as expenditure on gross national products, distribution of income, and general government revenue and expenditure.

Gulf handbook.
See item no. 41.

The Middle East and North Africa.
See item no. 56.

Middle East yearbook.
See item no. 57.

The economies of the Arab world: development since 1945.
See item no. 526.

Education in the Arab region viewed from the 1970 Marrakesh Conference.
See item no. 728.

Statistical summaries of educational development in the kingdom of Saudi Arabia, during the last five years: 1969/70-1973/74.
See item no. 731.

Education

724 Education in Saudi Arabia: a history of 15 years' effort to spread education in a developing country; an orthodox diagnosis and some proposals for a better future.

Abd-el Wahab, Abd-el Wassie. London: Macmillan, 1970. 76p. maps. bibliog.

725 First steps in grand design for education.

Tim Devlin. *The Times* (London), (23 Sept. 1976), p. VI.

726 Education: impressive achievements.

Arab Economist, no. 65, vol. 6 (June 1974), p. 67-9.

Education is of crucial importance to economic development, as Saudi Arabia's major handicap is the underdevelopment of its human resources. The article examines first the achievements to date, with a 300 per cent increase in student enrolment, moves for the education of women, and a campaign for the eradication of illiteracy. The second section deals with the expenditure on education, which has increased by about 800 per cent since 1963/64. It is acknowledged in conclusion that more can be done both quantitatively and qualitatively, especially with regard to the education of women, and vigorous development is needed in the field of kindergarten education, as an investment for the future. Also, more resources need to be put into technical and vocational education, which has not been very successful in Saudi Arabia, and more co-operation is obviously needed between the training establishments and the employers.

727 Education of women in Saudi Arabia.

Moslem World, vol. 46 (1956), p. 366-7.

Brief account of tentative steps towards the provision of education for women.

728 Education in the Arab region viewed from the 1970 Marrakesh Conference.
Muhammad Ahmad al-Ghannam. Paris: Unesco, 1971. 57p.
(Educational Studies & Documents, New Series, no. 1).
A statistical analysis of the problems of education in the Arab world, with financial details, types of school, age ranges, etc.

729 Education and science in the Arab world.
F. I. Qubain. Baltimore, Maryland; London: Johns Hopkins Press, 1966. 539p.
Very valuable work, treating the Arab world as a whole, but paying attention to developments in Saudi Arabia.

730 General summary of education in the kingdom of Saudi Arabia: 1973/4 (1393/4 AH).
Saudi Arabia. Ministry of Education. Riyadh: The Ministry, 1974.
Surveys the growth of education during the period in question, and indicates the pattern for future development.

731 Statistical summaries of educational development in the kingdom of Saudi Arabia, during the last five years: 1969/70-1973/74.
Saudi Arabia. Ministry of Education. Riyadh: The Ministry, 1974.
An extremely useful collection of statistics which demonstrate the growth of education at all levels in Saudi Arabia.

732 Schools complex at Riyadh.
Royal Institute of British Architects Journal, vol. 83, pt. 6 (1976), p. 247-8.
An account of the initial study, planning and design of a complex for over 3,000 pupils, including deaf, blind and mentally retarded children, from kindergarten to the secondary level of education.

733 Islamic education: its traditions and modernization into the Arab national systems.
Abdul Latif Tibawi. London: Luzac; New York: Crane Russak, 1972. 256p. bibliog.
Discusses the significance of Islam in its educative role, and demonstrates how Islamic principles have been incorporated into the secular part of the curriculum in Arab countries.

734 Modern education, Saudi Arabia.
George T. Trail, R. Bayly Winder. *History of Education Journal*, vol. 1, pt. 3 (1950), p. 121-33.
An examination of attempts to improve educational facilities in Saudi Arabia, with particular emphasis on the resistance from traditional forces to expansion of the scope of education.

735 Educational problems of Arab countries.
D. K. Wheeler. *International Review of Education*, vol. 12 (1966), p. 300-15.
An examination of educational problems with reference to the prime influences, such as technological change, on the development of education. The author examines the pattern of education, the problems caused by urbanization, cultural conflicts, and the lack of trained educators.

The Middle East: a handbook.
See item no. 24.

Arabian days.
See item no. 217.

The anatomy of the Saudi revolution.
See item no. 222.

The Bedouin.
See item no. 383.

Saudi Arabia today.
See item no. 460.

Administrative reform in Saudi Arabia.
See item no. 482.

National science and technology policies in the Arab states: present situation and future outlook.
See item no. 517.

Riyadh and the central province.
See item no. 518.

Saudi Arabia: investment opportunities.
See item no. 521.

Middle East oil money and its future expenditure.
See item no. 586.

Aspects of Saudi Arabia through the ages.
See item no. 740.

Literature and Art

736 **B D C mission visits Saudi Arabia: growth of the market likely.**
Bookseller, (13 Nov. 1976), p. 2460-1.
Discusses the possibility of sales of British books and bookselling expertise to Saudi Arabia.

737 **Artistic house decoration in Riyadh.**
V. Dickson.   *Man*, vol. 49 (1949), p. 76-7.
A look at the traditional forms of art used as distinctive methods of house decoration.

738 **Thoughts from the desert.**
Colin Eccleshone.   *Bookseller*, (20 Nov. 1976), p. 2534-6.
An assessment of the market potential for books and bookselling services in Saudi Arabia.

739 **The Middle East as a culture area.**
Raphael Patai.   *Middle East Journal*, vol. 6, pt. 1 (1952), p. 1-21.

740 **Aspects of Saudi Arabia through the ages.**
John J. Vianney.   *Levante*, vol. 13, pt. 3-4 (1966), p. 54-60.
The author emphasizes that although Saudi Arabia now looms large in world affairs because of oil, it should not be forgotten that its culture and literature in the past contributed significantly to the development of Western thought. He deals briefly with the oil industry and economic developments which have resulted from the oil revenues, and also considers the position of Saudi Arabia in Arab affairs, especially with regard to Arab regional co-operation.

Saudi Arabia: its people, its society, its culture.
See item no. 14.

The Middle East: a handbook.
See item no. 24.

The Bedouin.
See item no. 383.

A house built on sand: a political economy of Saudi Arabia.
See item no. 447.

Sports and Recreation

741 **Taif, city of colour.**
Frank T. Boylan. *Aramco World,* vol. 18, pt. 4 (1967), p. 34-7.

A description of Taif, which is situated in the mountains of the Hedjaz, and is the traditional summer residence of the population of the coastal region. Developments are now taking place to exploit the leisure aspects of the city, especially in the light of the increasing wealth and leisure of the consumer society which is now developing in Saudi Arabia and which, of course, also exists within the expatriate community.

742 **Sports and leisure centre, Jeddah.**
Royal Institute of British Architects Journal, vol. 83, pt. 6 (1976), p. 245-6.

The sport and leisure centre complex was designed against a rigid timetable, which required contract documentation after 180 calendar days, and this article describes the original planning and design of the complex.

743 **The Saudis go for goal.**
Sam Younger. *Middle East International,* no. 74 (July 1977), p. 28-9.

Account of the Saudi Arabian plans to improve the standard and status of association football, using the English expert Jimmy Hill as a consultant. The scheme involves structuring a league programme and instituting a national youth policy as an investment for the future.

Riyadh and the central province.
See item no. 518.

The Press

General

Saudi Arabia.
See item no. 15.

The Middle East: a handbook.
See item no. 24.

The Middle East and North Africa.
See item no. 56.

Dailies

744 al-Bilad.
  Jeddah (King Abdul Aziz St.), 1934-
Published in Arabic.

745 al-Jazirah.
  Riyadh (P.O.B. 354, Apt. 88, Municipality Building, Safat).
Published in Arabic.

746 al-Madina al-Munawara.
  Jeddah (P.O.B. 807), 1937-
Published in Arabic.

The Press. Weeklies

747 al-Nadwah.
Mecca, 1958-
Published in Arabic.

748 Replica.
Jeddah (P.O.B. 2043).
Published in English, and based on the content of Saudi newspapers and broadcasts.

749 al-Riyadh.
Riyadh (P.O.B. 851).
Published in Arabic.

750 Saudi Gazette.
Jeddah (Al Mina St., P.O.B. 5576), 1975-
Published in English.

751 al-Ukadh.
Jeddah.
Published in Arabic, and has a limited circulation.

Weeklies

752 Akhbar al-Dhahran.
Dammam, 1958-
Published in Arabic.

753 al-Dawa.
Riyadh.
Published in Arabic.

754 Arabian Sun.
Dhahran: Aramco.
In English, published by the oil company.

755 News from Saudi Arabia.
Jeddah: Press Dept., Ministry of Information, 1961-
Publishes news bulletins in English.

756 News of the Muslim World.
Mecca: Muslim World League.
Published in Arabic.

757 Oil Caravan Weekly.
Dhahran: Aramco.
In Arabic, published by the oil company.

758 al-Qasim.
Riyadh, 1959-

759 al-Riyadh.
Mecca, 1960-
Aimed at young men.

760 Umm al-Qura.
Mecca: The Government, 1924-
Published by the government, and dealing with governmental, industrial and social
affairs.

761 al-Yamamah.
Riyadh (P.O.B. 851), 1952-

762 al-Yaum.
Dammam (P.O.B. 565), 1965-

Periodicals

763 al-Manhal.
Jeddah (44 Arafat St.), 1937-
A literary monthly.

764 al-Mujtama.
Riyadh (P.O.B. 354, Apt. 88, Municipality Building, Safat),
1964-
An Arabic weekly.

765 **al-Tijarah.**
Jeddah, 1960-
A monthly for businessmen.

766 **Hajj.**
Mecca: Ministry of Pilgrimage and Endowments, 1947-
Published in Arabic and English.

Bibliographies

767 The States of the Arabian peninsula and the Gulf littoral: a selected bibliography.
Compiled by John Duke Anthony.   Washington, D.C.: Middle East Institute, 1973. 21p.

The emphasis in this bibliography is on material pertinent to systems of government, politics, international relations and economies. The entries are partially annotated and divided into two main sections, the first dealing with books, monographs, pamphlets and proceedings, and the second listing periodical articles.

768 The contemporary Middle East, 1948-1973: a selective and annotated bibliography.
Compiled by George N. Atiyah.   Boston, Massachusetts: G. K. Hall, 1975. 664p. (Series Seventy).

This work is basically concerned with the social sciences, with a small section on the arts and literature. Emphasis is placed on general works, bibliographies, history, politics, social conditions, education and economic conditions, and both monographs and periodical articles are included. The sections of relevance to Saudi Arabia are those covering the Middle East, the Arab countries in general, and the specific section on Saudi Arabia in the Arabian peninsula section. Annotations are provided essentially to indicate the contents of each volume and article, and evaluations are only given in a very few cases. The index is alphabetical by author, place and concept; references are to entry numbers.

769 Soviet Middle East studies: an analysis and bibliography.
Alexander Rollo Colin Bolton.   London: Oxford University Press for the Royal Institute of International Affairs, 1959. 8 parts.

This work covers current affairs, history, and economics; part 1 is concerned with the Arabian peninsula.

770 Arab culture and society in change: a partially annotated bibliography of books and articles in English, French, German and Italian.

Centre for the Study of the Modern Arab World. Beirut: Dar el-Mashreq, 1973. 318p.

The bibliography is the result of material assembled for various research projects carried out at the Centre at St. Joseph's University, Beirut. The area covered by this work is the Arab countries of the Middle East and North Africa from the First World War to the end of 1971. The theme of the work 'is the encounter which is and has been taking place in Arab society between the values and concepts of modern or Western culture, and those traditional values and concepts which have formed Arab consciousness and society'. The bibliography comprises fifteen main subject divions; entries are numbered, and the author, regional, and selected subject indexes refer to those numbers.

771 The emergence of Arab nationalism from the 19th century to 1921.

Frank A. Clements. London: Diploma Press, 1976. 290p.

An annotated bibliography, not all of which is relevant to Saudi Arabia. Only works in English or translated into English are included. The work is arranged by subject with each subject area having its own introductory essay: 1. The struggle between the Arabs and Turks: a. Ottoman administration and aspects of diplomacy; b. The beginnings of the Arab nationalist movement; c. The arab revolt and war in the Middle East. 2. The peace settlement and its consequences: a. Arab case at the peace conference and the resultant settlement; b. Rivalry between Hussein and Ibn Saud; c. Arab reaction to the Palestine mandate; d. The Cairo Conference of 1921. 3. The fertile crescent under the mandate system.

772 T. E. Lawrence: a reader's guide.

Frank A. Clements. Newton Abbot, England: David & Charles, 1972; Hamden, Connecticut: Shoe String Press, 1973. 208p.

An annotated bibliography of works by and about T. E. Lawrence, with the relevant entries scattered throughout the sections. In this context the areas of relevance are the attitudes of Lawrence and the Arab Bureau to Ibn Saud, and the difficulties with Sherif Hussein following the peace settlement.

773 Foreign affairs bibliography: a selected and annotated list of books on international relations.

Council on Foreign Relations. New York: Council on Foreign Relations, 1933-, in progress.

A general, classified listing of books dealing with international relations. The publication cumulates at ten-yearly intervals.

774 An Arabian bibliography.

Gerald De Gaury. *Royal Central Asian Society Journal*, vol. 31, pts. 3-4 (1944), p. 315-20.

An enumerative history of Western-language books and articles on Saudi Arabia, the pilgrimage to Mecca, and connected subjects. The list is prefaced by a brief introduction to Saudi Arabia, and some of the earliest historical accounts by European travellers.

775 A bibliography of articles on the Middle East.
Compiled by Uri Dotan, Arigdor Levy. Tel Aviv, Israel: The University, 1970. 227p.

A series of bibliographies, originally begun by the Hebrew University of Jerusalem, beginning in 1954 with entries dating from 1939. Author index only.

776 Problems of the Near East.
Edited by Edward Mead Earle. Washington, D.C.: Carnegie Endowment for International Peace, 1924. 23p. (International Relations Club Bibliography Series, no. 2).

A narrative bibliography covering the period to the peace settlement after World War I. The work includes Saudi Arabia and is divided into the following sections: 1. General works of reference on the Near East; 2. Historical and economic geography of the Near East; 3. Western imperialism in the Near East; 4. The rise of nationalism in the Near East; 5. Religious problems of the Near East; 6. The Near East in the World War; 7. The Near East since the Armistice of 1918; 8. American interests in the Near East; 9. Periodical literature. Briefly annotated, dated, and mainly confined to material held in American libraries.

777 A selected and annotated bibliography of books and periodicals in Western languages dealing with the Near and Middle East, with special emphasis on medieval and modern times; with supplement.
Edited by Richard Ettinghausen. Washington, D.C.: Middle East Institute, 1953. 137p.

A classified, annotated bibliography with author indexes. It contains about 2,000 entries for books, maps and serials.

778 Analytical guide to the bibliographies on the Arabian peninsula.
C. L. Geddes. Denver, Colorado: American Institute of Islamic Studies, 1974. 50p.

A listing of some seventy bibliographies in European languages on the Arabian peninsula, together with annotations as to coverage, content, limitations, etc. Those dealing solely with Saudi Arabia are numbers 3, 6, 12, 16, 18, 26, 30, 36, 43, 44, 51, 56, 57, 59, 60, 62, 63 and 69.

779 Maps and atlases of the Middle East.
Gerry A. Hale. *Middle East Studies Association Bulletin*, vol. 3, pt. 3 (1969), p. 17-39.

An article primarily aimed at surveying the teaching materials available on the Middle East, covering general and specialist maps and atlases of the area, with an indication as to scope and content.

Bibliographies

780 Bibliography of the Arabian peninsula.
Harry W. Hazard. New Haven, Connecticut: Human Relations Area Files Press, 1956. 256p.

A useful listing, produced by the American Geographical Society, of books and articles, classified by subject. No index.

781 A selected bibliography of articles dealing with the Middle East.
Hebrew University. Economic Research Institute. Jerusalem: Hebrew University, 1939-, in progress.

The first volume covered 1939-1950, and thereafter coverage was for three-year periods, selection being from journals available in Israeli libraries. Entries are arranged by country, with general sections covering the Middle East and Arabian peninsula. Each section is further subdivided by topic. Entries are not annotated but give author, title, and journal references. The index is by author only.

782 The Arabian peninsula: society and politics.
Edited by Derek Hopwood. London: Allen & Unwin; Lotowa, New Jersey: Rowman & Littlefield, 1972. 320p.

In his bibliographical survey 'Some western studies of Saudi Arabia, Yemen and Aden', the editor examines the type and range of literature available, with particular reference to contributions by Western writers (since World War II) dealing with contemporary affairs and the Philby case. Other essays in the book are dealt with under the appropriate headings.

783 Middle East and Islam: a bibliographical introduction.
Edited by Derek Hopwood, Diana Grimwood-Jones. Zug, Switzerland: Inter-Documentation Co.; New York: International Publications Service, 1972. 368p. (Middle East Libraries Committee. Biblioteca Asiatica, no. 9).

The object of the work is to provide an introduction to the subject and it is often deliberately selective to reduce the whole to manageable proportions. Each section is the contribution of a specialist and reflects his tastes and interests. As a general rule works in non-European languages are excluded, except where no satisfactory European work exists or where Arabic material is essential. The work is divided into the following sections: 1. Reference; 2. Islamic studies; 3. Subject bibliographies; 4. Regional bibliographies; 5. Arabic language and literature. Some sections are listings with introductory essays, others annotated lists, and the remainder texts in which the items are included.

784 Economic history of the Middle East to 1914.
Charles P. Issawi. *Middle East Studies Association Bulletin*, vol. 2, pt. ii (1968), p. 1-14.

A bibliographical introduction to material available on the economic history of the area divided into the following sections: 1. The Islamic period to 1500 A.D.; 2. 1500-1800; 3. 1800-1918; 4. Ottoman empire; 5. Egypt; 6. Sudan; 7. Arab Asia; 8. Iran. The author makes no claim to completeness and states that the present state of knowledge is best described as a bunch of holes tied together with string. 'The trouble is that, here, the holes are so wide that rather large fish can easily slip through, while the string is so weak that one cannot be sure of keeping what one thinks one holds'.

785 Bibliography of the Arabian peninsula.
Eric Macro. Miami, Florida: University of Miami Press, 1958.
80p.

A useful listing of some 2,000 relevant items covering all aspects of the area, though the political content is minimal. Entries are arranged alphabetically by author, with anonymous works arranged by title under the heading 'anonymous'. Entries include books, periodicals and works from official sources, regardless of language. No subject index.

786 Index Islamicus 1906-1955.
Compiled by J. D. Pearson. Cambridge, England: Heffer,
1958. 897p. New ed., London: Mansell, 1972. (Distributed in
the U.S.A. by International Scholarly Book Services, Forest
Grove, Oregon).

A catalogue of articles on Islamic subjects in periodicals, Festschriften, congresses and other collective works. The work is arranged by subjects, dealing first with general material, and then with subjects under general headings such as Art, Religion, and Literature. Further sections are devoted to area studies subdivided by subject, and each subject is given a running number which is the point of reference from the index. Entries are not annotated, but give author, title, bibliographical details and cross-references to other entries. Supplements are now being produced annually and the index has been changed to refer to the main subject number and sub-division number rather than to entry numbers.

787 Literature on the kingdom of Saudi Arabia.
George Rentz. *Middle East Journal*, vol. 4, pt. 2 (1950), p.
244-9.

In spite of its date this review article continues to provide a good starting point for any study of the subject.

788 A selected and annotated bibliography of economic literature on the Arab countries of the Middle East, 1953-1965.
Beirut: American University of Beirut, 1967. 458p.

An annotated bibliography of some 5,500 items arranged by country and subject. The section on Saudi Arabia (p. 267-84) comprises some 223 items under the following headings: General; Population and labour; Development plans; Agriculture; Industry; Mining; Transport and communications; International relations; Money and banking; Public finance.

789 Recent Arab literature on Arabism.
Nicola A. Ziadeh. *Middle East Journal*, vol. 6, pt. 4 (1952),
p. 468-73.

A review article which discusses recent Arab literature by providing a summary of the development of Arab nationalism. Consideration is given to developments in the 19th century, the First World War and the Arab revolt. The author also considers the political boundaries of the Arab states and the relationship between Arabism and Pan-Islamism.

Index

The index is a single alphabetical sequence of authors (personal and corporate), titles of publications (excluding articles in periodicals), and subjects. Index entries refer both to the main items and to other works mentioned in the notes to each item. Title entries are in italics. Numeration refers to the items as numbered.

169

171

F

oil industry 712, 715
wage structure 714
Labour law and practice in the kingdom of Saudi Arabia 716
Lackner, H. 447
Laffin, J. 384
Lancaster, W. O. 448–449
Land of the Arabs 507
Land tenure 142, 507, 665
Land utilization 142, 178
Landau, J. 411
Landen, R. G. 49
Language 16, 35, 384
  bibliographies 783
Lapidus, I. M. 450
Laqueur, W. 344
Large international firm in developing countries: the international petroleum industry 556
Lateef, A. 345
Lateef, N. A. 652
Law 476, 481
  banks and banking 519
  commercial 511
  Islamic 476, 478, 480
  labour 716
Law of oil concessions in the Middle East and North Africa 583
Lawrence, T. E. 85, 209, 216, 249, 259–262, 289–291, 295
  bibliographies 772
  negotiations with Hussein 280
Leachman, G. 111
League of Arab States 282
Leatherdale, J. 150
Leblicker, R. 12
Leeman, W. A. 546
Lees, G. M. 570
Legal framework for oil concessions in the Arab world 600
Leipold, L. E. 13
Leisure centres 742
Leisure provision 741
Lenczowski, G. 50, 451, 547, 588, 610
Lesch, A. M. 363
Letters of Gertrude Lothian Bell. Vol. 2 251
Letters of T. E. Lawrence 259
Levy, A. 775
Lewis, B. 51, 229
Lewis, C. C. 292
Linnean Society 184, 191
Lipsky, G. A. 14
Liquified petroleum gas
  nationalization 599

Literacy 24, 726
Literature 24, 384, 740
  bibliographies 768, 783, 786
Little, I. M. D. 589
Living conditions 6, 11
  foreign employees 18
Liwa
  travellers' accounts 126
Locust control 96, 126, 136, 658, 668
Long, D. E. 15, 479
Longrigg, S. H. 52, 452, 571
Lord of Arabia: Ibn Saud, an intimate study of a king 193
Lorimer, J. G. 53

M

Mabro, R. 589–590
Macdowell, I. 175, 695
McFarlane, J. 88
McGinnies, W. G. 151
McGregor, R. 420
Mackie, J. B. 653
McLachlan, K. 592
McLoughlin, S. 696
McMahon, Sir Henry 255, 287
Macro, E. 785
Maddox, J. 548
Magazines 41, 752–766
Major companies of the Arab world 29
Maker of modern Arabia 212
Malone, J. J. 206, 393
Mandate system
  bibliographies 771
Mandaville, J. 176
Manners and customs of the Rwala Bedouins 385
Manpower and oil in Arab countries 581
Manpower problems 368
Mansfield, P. 54–55, 230
Maps and mapping 16, 146, 150, 154, 180–182
  early period 97
  Hedjaz 117
  Middle East 57, 779
  oil industry 57
  water resources 178
March arabesque 31
Marine industries 621
Marine trade 710
Maritime affairs 352
Marlowe, J. 346
Marxism 337, 345

183

revenue 536, 538, 552, 606
revenue-surplus funds disposal 63, 325,
  495, 502, 504, 534, 586, 589–590,
  592–593, 598, 612
Rub' al Khali-exploration 576
social implications 142
statistics 57, 718, 720
supertankers 703
tax-OPEC 598
topographical aspects 551
training programmes 540, 586–587,
  617
USA-foreign investments 602
Oil, the Middle East and the world 544
Oil, power and politics: conflict in
  Arabia, the Red Sea and the
  Gulf 311
Oil production, revenues and economic
  development prospects for
  Iran...Saudi Arabia... Bahrain 552
Oil refineries
nationalization 599
Oil reserves
conservation 563, 598, 610
discovery 36, 50, 200
nationalization 599
offshore-exploitation 578
offshore-legislation 578
Oil sheikhs 432
Oil tankers 597, 703
Oilfields 561, 570
Oilfields, Offshore 567
development 578
legislation 578
Oman 154, 311, 356
boundaries 54, 326, 339–340, 342,
  347–348, 351, 364, 369, 373
Dhofar region 328
travellers' accounts 100
Onassis tanker dispute 597
OPEC 504, 541, 548, 558, 563, 613
aid programmes 531
common production policy 549
history and development 554, 611
member countries-statistics 553
policy 554
political aspects 560
price controls 605, 607–608, 611
tax control 598
OPEC and the petroleum industry 554
Operation Bultiste 622
Organization of Petroleum Exporting
  Countries 553
Orientations 301
Ornithology 183

Orrmont, A. 91
Ostama 211

P

Paleozoic arch 143
Palestine and the Arabs 303
Palestine liberation movements 318, 355
Palestine Liberation Organization 363
Palestine mandate
  Arab reaction-bibliographies 771
Palgrave, William Gifford 77, 92
Pan-Islamism
  bibliographies 789
Parker, J. B. 656–657
Parr, P. J. 208
Partition of Turkey: a diplomatic history,
  1913-1923 284
Pastoralism 142, 389
Pasture development 651
Patai, R. 455, 739
Patwardhan, V. N. 473
Pauling, H. C. 713
Pauling, H. R. 712
Peace settlement
  World War I-Arabia-bibliographies 771
Pearl fishing 621
Pearson, J. D. 786
Peck, M. 356
Pelly, Sir L. 93
Pendleton, M. and O. 18
Penetration of Arabia: a record of the
  development of Western knowledge
  concerning the Arabian
  peninsula 89
Penrose, E. T. 555–558
Peppelenbasch, P. G. N. 456
Peretz, D. 60
Periodicals 41, 752–766
Permanent sovereignty over oil
  resources: a study of Middle East
  oil concessions and legal
  change 596
Persian Gulf in the twentieth century 346
Personal narrative of a pilgrimage to el
  Madinah and Meccah 84
Pesce, A. 61, 674
Petrochemicals industries 540, 618, 620
training 711
Petroleum statistical bulletin 718
Petromin 512, 540, 559
Petromin University 540

187

191

Map of Saudi Arabia

This map shows the more important towns and other features mentioned in the text.

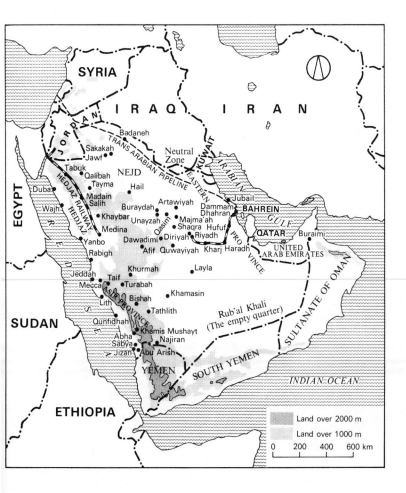